GOLF

PLAY TO WIN

GOLF

DAVID FEHERTY
ALAN FINE

OCTOPUS BOOKS

First published in 1987 by
Octopus Books Limited
59 Grosvenor Street
London W1

© Octopus Books Limited, 1987
All rights reserved.
ISBN 0-7064-2862-5

Design by Laurence Bradbury Design Associates
Assisted by Sarah Collins

Colour artwork by Mulkern Rutherford Studio
Line illustrations by Klim Forster
Cartoons by Anni Axworthy

Art editor: Jeremy Bratt
Project editor: Tessa Rose
Copy-editor: Diana Vowles
Production: Peter Thompson

Typeset by SX Composing, Rayleigh, Essex
Colour origination by Mandarin, Hong Kong
Printed in Hong Kong

CONTENTS

ACKNOWLEDGEMENTS

We would like to say thank you to some people who, each in their individual way, helped us to complete this book – sometimes in spite of ourselves!

Mrs Edwards at Bridgeview Physiotherapy Clinic for her help with the warm up exercises.
Sue Bamford and Claire Fish for checking and typing the text.
Tessa Rose of Octopus for giving us the opportunity to communicate our ideas.

For David: David Jones and Phil Ritson for their expert guidance, and Caroline, my wife – the biggest help I have ever had.

For Alan: Timothy Gallwey, Graham Alexander, John Whitmore and Penny Newman, each of whom taught me how to go beyond what I thought possible.

When David and I were asked to write a book on golf we thought it a wonderful idea. Here was a chance for us to communicate our ideas on paper. Neither of us had written a book before and we quickly discovered that the written word is a more difficult medium than the spoken word. Now, of course, after many hours of meetings, thousands of words, and the burning of much midnight oil, we are a little more appreciative of the skills of experienced writers.

Our book is aimed to give the beginner a solid start to the game and plenty to continue with, and the more advanced player some check points for his or her game and further food for thought (or not thinking, as you will see!). We have deliberately tried to keep away from complicated analysis of the swing, believing that it creates more problems than it solves. We have also tried to keep in mind that golf should be fun. Some of the theories of learning contained in this book were very helpful to us in its creation.

By writing this book together, we have drawn on different sets of experiences. David has been playing golf since he was 10 years old, and turned professional in 1976 at the age of 17. Since then he has worked his way through the ranks, starting as an Assistant Pro and graduating to the tour in 1979. The season of 1986 has been his best to date, with the Italian and Scottish Open titles to his credit. Both these were won in sudden-death play offs, so he is no stranger to competing under pressure.

I developed an interest in the way people learn and how some people realize more of their potential than others. Through studying the theories of Timothy Gallwey's Inner Game and other associated approaches to learning, I became involved in many different fields of activity. I now enjoy the pleasure and privilege of sharing what I have learned with sports people, from beginners to world ranks, and from musicians to international businessmen.

As the book progressed we discovered we had much to learn about golf and writing. We sincerely hope that both golf and this book will be for you what they have been for us; a source of fun, learning and achievement.

Alan Fine

ANCIENT ADDICTION

There's a very old joke about the golfer who, when asked by a beauty queen if he'd like to 'play around', replied, 'Certainly, but I haven't brought my clubs with me!' How many of us have been consumed by this game to the point where we can't get it out of our minds?

Why do we play?

The object of the game of golf according to the rules is to hit the ball around the 18 holes of the golf course from tee into hole in the fewest possible shots. But why do we do this? What do we gain?

Well, the most common reasons for playing are: the challenge and excitement of achievement; to get exercise; to make business connections (or even deals!); and to get away from everything and everyone (you can play on your own). From all of these come satisfaction and fulfilment.

It's a game that looks easy. The ball doesn't move – and you've got ages in which to hit the thing. Yet stories abound of golfers who have ended up breaking their clubs in frustration.

There are several factors in golf that combine to make it the challenging, interesting and addictive game that it is.

The precision

Compared with other sports the clubhead and ball are small, thus requiring some skill to bring them together. Add to that the fact that the clubhead has to travel quite a long way to get to the ball and covers this distance at speed. This means that it can be tricky to correct errors in the way the clubhead is travelling. By the time the player has tried to correct the error the club has already struck the ball. Finally, the ball often has to be hit over 200yd. A ball that leaves the clubhead slightly off line can be as much as 50yd off target by the time it comes to rest. Also, there's the effect of spin.

The design of the course

The course is usually designed to make playing more challenging, or frustrating, depending on your point of view. Course designers work out to where Mr Average is most likely to hit the ball and then put a bunker, or pond, or a clump of trees in that spot. Those of you who have played any golf will have noticed an additional law of nature at work on golf courses. The more you want your ball to go somewhere the further away from that spot it goes. Conversely, the more you want your ball to avoid a particular spot, the more it seems to be attracted there!

Rules and etiquette

Golf has a set of rules that can change depending on where you play, when you play (i.e. weather conditions) and the condition of the course. It also has several different systems of scoring and a handicapping system which means that very good players can play against not so good players and still have a close contest.

Although not actually in the rules, there is an accepted code of behaviour in golf. Break this code and the penalties range from being glared at by other golfers to being barred from the course by the club committee. Examples of etiquette are raking the sand in a bunker you have played out of, and not moving or talking as someone is about to play.

What makes golf different

Unlike most sports, you don't usually play against your opponent. Your opponent cannot do anything to make the game more difficult for you, so in a sense you are playing against yourself. You cannot blame anyone when you make a mistake – and you can take all the credit when you play well.

Unless you are aiming to get into the Guinness Book of Records, it takes about 3½ hours to play a round of golf. Making a generous allowance of 10 seconds for each shot and 150 shots per round (very generous) you don't have to be a mathematician to discover that most of the time spent playing golf isn't in hitting the ball.

All these factors combine to make golf a sport like no other and deserving of its title 'The Royal and Ancient Game of Golf'. The millions of people of all ages playing the game worldwide testify to this.

Having said all this, let's say right now: GOLF CAN BE EASY AND ENJOYABLE.

That winning feeling: David Feherty holes a 45 foot putt at the second play off hole to seal victory in the 1986 Bell's Scottish Open.

THE EQUIPMENT

THE CLUBS

Read any golf magazine and you will see advertisements for equipment leaping out at you from the pages. There's so much variety and so much high technology available these days you can get spoilt for choice. Let's first look at what's essential.

Types of club

The rules of golf allow a maximum of 14 clubs in your bag when you are actually playing. Every club will hit the ball a different distance, and this distance is governed (assuming the swing is the same) by the angle of the face of the club as it meets the ball – known as the loft. Each club has a number on its sole which signifies the amount of loft that it has. The lower the number the less the loft and the further the club will hit the ball.

Simply described, each club has a grip made of rubber, or occasionally leather, a shaft made of steel and/or graphite (you'll occasionally find an old club made of wood) and a clubhead made of steel or wood.

The clubs are divided into three types:
Woods. So named because the clubhead was originally made of wood. These days you will also find metal or very occasionally even graphite headed woods. The number 1 wood or driver is usually used to hit the ball off the tee. Woods are commonly numbered 1 to 5, although occasionally you will find woods numbered as high as 9 or 10 but these are rare. 3, 4 and 5 woods are known as fairway woods.
Irons. Here the clubheads are made of metal and are numbered 1 to 9, and then PW and SW, for pitching wedge and sand wedge respectively. The sand wedge is shaped differently from the other irons. It has a broader sole to prevent it from getting buried too deeply in the sand, making bunker shots easier to play.
Putter. The putter has almost no loft and is used on or just off the green when the ground is flat and smooth.

Many beginners will start with a half set of clubs, eg driver and 4 wood, 4, 6, 8 irons, a wedge and a putter, which is perfectly adequate to get started with.

There is an enormous variety of putters on the market. The blade comes in many shapes and sizes; small or large, some with flanges, others are offset. Most have the shaft attached to the heel of the blade, some to the centre and, occasionally, the toe. Try them out – most pro shops will let you. Whichever type feels best and produces results is the one for you.

The shafts of clubs are made with various degrees of flex. They are generally classified as S – stiff; R – regular; L – ladies; but this can vary, so ask your pro for the right one.

Choosing clubs

The most important factor of all when choosing clubs is that they have to *feel right for you.* There will always be people, especially manufacturers, making all kinds of claims for their clubs. It's a personal decision and you have to

Below left: **A typical 1 wood or driver.**
Middle: **All irons share the same basic shape but the loft varies. (See diagram showing trajectories, opposite.)**
Right: **One of the many types of putter. They all work!**

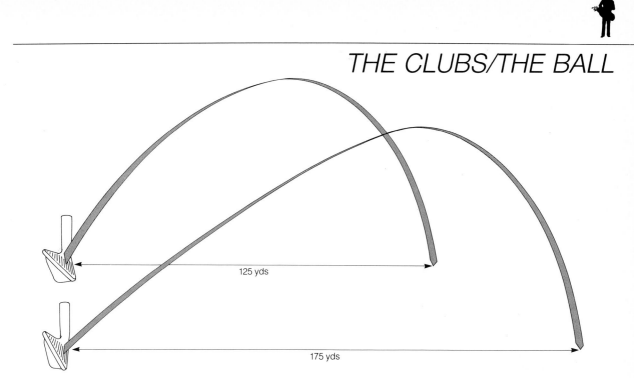

125 yds

175 yds

be happy with them. Here are some points to look out for when making your selection.

Price

You first need to consider how much you want to spend. The most economical purchase will be a second hand half set of clubs. Many pros (particularly at busy public courses) have second hand clubs for sale. They often sell clubs and take an old set in part exchange. At the other end of the scale would be custom-made clubs.

The lie of the club

The angle between the blade and the shaft is known as the lie of the club. If the angle is too large you are likely to catch the toe of the club on the ground at impact. If the angle is too small you may catch the heel. The lie of an iron can be checked quite simply as shown in the illustration. Always use a hard, flat surface, such as a paving stone, when using this test. The lie of an iron can be altered by a good club repairer, but the lie of a wood is almost impossible to change.

The flex

This depends on your play. Without going into the physics involved, the more clubhead speed you can generate the stiffer the shafts you should use. A regular shaft would be most appropriate for most handicap players.

Care of clubs

Most golfers put headcovers on their woods to protect the clubheads. Some also use covers on their irons but this is much rarer. You should dry your clubs off carefully if they become wet, wiping off any grass, sand or mud that accumulates on the head. When rubber grips become dirty they can be washed with soap and water. It they become shiny you can get your local pro to change them.

The ball

It often looks as if there are two types: yours, which usually misses the hole, and your part-

Above: The face of a 9 iron (top) is more lofted than that of a 4 iron (bottom), thus giving a higher trajectory and a shorter flight.

Left: A good guide as to whether your club has the correct lie for you is that a thick coin will just fit under the 'toe' when you address the ball comfortably.

PERSONAL ITEMS

ner's, which goes in! But there are actually two types of construction.

Wound balls have elastic wound very tightly around a circular core inside them. There are two coverings, surlyn, which is tougher and resists cutting when the ball is mishit, and balata, which is softer, gives more feel but cuts more easily.

Solid balls are made from a solid rubber core with a tough plastic outer cover that is almost impossible to cut.

Most pro shops sell balls that have been rejected as sub-standard. They are therefore less expensive than a perfect ball and an ideal way to begin playing the game.

Gloves

Many golfers wear a leather glove on their left hand. This is because as they swing the club there can be a lot of friction between their left hand and the club (assuming that they play right handed). You'll soon know whether you need one. If you choose to wear one it should be as tight as possible, but comfortable.

Shoes

Golf shoes have spikes to minimize any dangers of slipping. Some shoes have lots of small rubber pimples (instead of spikes), which make walking off the course much more comfortable but don't give quite the same grip. Given that you will have to walk several miles when you play a round of golf, it's important that your shoes are right.

Bag

These come in various shapes and sizes. Generally speaking, the bigger the bag the heavier it is to carry, so be careful if you're feeling rich. You can hire (or buy) trollies on which you can wheel your bag if you don't like to carry it.

Clothing

As in all sports, there is a fashion in golf. Go to any golf course and you will see what's in vogue. What is essential is that your clothing allows you to swing freely and is neither too hot nor too cold. Payne Stewart, illustrated opposite, is a good example of the fashion consciousness that can be seen on golf courses around the world. The variety of styles and the general 'stylishness' in this respect adds to the attractiveness of the game.

Ball marker

You will use this when your ball lies between your partner's and the hole when you are both on the green. You will mark the position of your ball with the marker and pick your ball up, so that it doesn't obstruct the path of your partner's ball.

Tees

You can place your ball on a tee for the first shot only at any hole (most amateurs use a tee for all first shots). It makes it much easier to use a driver (you'll see). Pros sometimes don't employ them when using irons on shorter holes. You can buy wooden or plastic tees of different lengths; some plastic tees are made so that they can only be pushed a set distance into the ground. This means that the ball is always teed up to the same height.

Pitch mark repairer

When your ball lands on the green it will very likely cause a dent. You use this tool to repair the damage to the surface of the green.

We haven't included emergency equipment in this list. This includes a hip flask, Mars bar, the notes from your last lesson, a set of course rules, and a copy of *101 Excuses for Being Home Late from the Golf Course*!

FIRST GEAR

"Very expensive equipment is often no better than reasonably priced gear, and in most cases you are paying for a name rather than quality in terms of performance. The chrome on expensive clubs rusts just as quickly as that of moderately priced ones. So, after a round, don't just throw your clubs into the boot of the car and forget about them until your next outing. If you want to take care of your game, take care of your clubs" – *David Feherty*

Just as styles of play vary from golfer to golfer, so do styles of dress. Payne Stewart always cuts a dash on the fairways with his Roaring Twenties outfits.

MAKING LEARNING EASY

THE CONSTRUCTIVE APPROACH

Golf can be easy to learn and easy to play if you take the right approach. Many golfers get into difficulties because the attitude that they take on to the practice range or the golf course is a destructive one. The way you think about the game can at best make it simple and enjoyable and at worst make it frustrating and difficult.

Understanding a little bit about the process of learning can make all the knowledge you will gain about how to play the game much easier to put into effect, and can help you avoid some of the pitfalls that the unwary golfer can fall into. This chapter explores some of the common mistakes made as people try to improve, and how to prevent them.

Trying too hard

The harder you try the worse you get and the worse you get the harder you try – one of the most common problems encountered in the game of golf.

What is meant by trying too hard? It means thinking too much about what you are trying to do; criticizing yourself when you don't do it correctly; and putting more physical effort

than is necessary into the shot. All of these cause you to tighten your muscles. The tighter your muscles the more difficult it is to swing correctly. When you don't swing correctly the ball doesn't go where you want it to. So then you try harder, which causes more muscle tightening and so on into a vicious circle.

Biting off more than you can chew

When you watch professional golfers you probably marvel at the effortless way they hit the ball huge distances with uncanny accuracy. They are wonderful models to copy. Problems arise when instead of using them as a guide you actually attempt to hit the ball the same distance, with the same accuracy, and with the same swing, trying to make an improvement in the space of a day or a week or a month that the pro took years to perfect. When you don't succeed you become disappointed, frustrated and eventually lose confidence in yourself.

What you are doing is setting goals that are too high for you at that time. When your goals are unrealistically high, you will fail to achieve them. Of course it is important to aim high in order to improve but this must be tempered with realism.

Negative self-images

Sometimes you may play golf with the idea that you really aren't very good or that everyone else is better than you. When you are in this frame of mind the bunkers look like enormous chasms, water hazards look like oceans, and greens look as if they are the size of a postage stamp. Partners and opponents all look much more confident and relaxed than you do. Your image of yourself is very negative. If you hit a good shot you think it must have been luck because you believe that you simply aren't good enough to have hit that particular shot.

A poor self-image can cause more problems than any other factor in the game.

Too much emphasis on results

You know you've fallen into this trap when you can't think of anything other than your bad shots, and you've stopped enjoying the game.

Over-trying is counter-productive.

Two sides of the same coin: negative and positive self-images.

We play golf for many reasons, some of which are mentioned in the previous chapter. In all of these factors is enjoyment. In this relaxed state of mind it is very easy to learn, and so performance improves very quickly. You like the way you are playing, but when you eventually have an off day you start to get concerned about your standard. When this happens your mind becomes busy, your learning rate slows down and the enjoyment goes out of the game. Good performance (or good results if you prefer) is created by being in a relaxed state of mind, the foundation for speedy learning.

Each of us has an ability to learn that is rarely made the best use of. Children are very fast learners because they haven't yet been conditioned to 'try hard' or develop poor images of themselves. (Why we become conditioned would need another book.)

Just as there are some basics to the technique of golf there are some basics to the technique of learning, so here are a few to get you on your way.

One thing at a time

You can only consciously concentrate on one thing at a time. If you try to think of too many things at once the effect will be counter-productive and will only serve to confuse you. Not only is it not necessary to try to think of everything at once, it's not possible. Although a golf swing is a complex set of movements, most of them happen subconsciously.

When you learnt to ride a bicycle you didn't try to think of all the different movements involved. You got on it, found out what it felt like, had a few wobbles but kept on doing it until you found out how. All you knew consciously was that you wanted to ride without wobbling and falling off. Your subconscious took care of all the movements.

So it is with golf. Your subconscious will take over. What you have to do is concentrate on one thing at a time.

Concentration

Relaxed concentration is the key to success in anything. Nothing worthwhile was ever achieved without it. Watch any great golfer at any level in the game. Although they all seem to swing differently, they all show excellent concentration.

To attain this state you need to become interested in what you are doing. Concentrating on something is easy when you are interested in it. You never have to 'try' and concentrate on an exciting TV programme or a good book. So whatever you are doing, whether it's practice or playing, make it as interesting as possible.

Many people concentrate too much on what they should be doing and what they shouldn't have done, and as a result never really know what they *are* actually doing. What you are about to do is in the future and what you should have done is in the past. What you are actually doing right now is what will affect the ball and it's the starting point for improving. If you can't tell what you are actually doing at the outset, how will you change it?

CONTROL/GOAL-SETTING

Practice 'feel'

Being able to 'feel' what you are doing means being able to sense how your body does what it does when you swing. It's the secret to control. It's also impossible to put into words how something feels. No words can really describe what it is like to parachute from an aeroplane, and nor can they really describe the feel of a golf swing.

To develop 'feel' you must practise sensing your movements without trying to alter them. You must also forget about where the ball is going for a while.

One thing that will prevent you from gaining this 'feel' of what you are doing is thinking too much about what you are trying to achieve. Because you can only consciously concentrate on one thing at a time you can either think about what you should be doing, or feel what you actually are doing, but not both together. Another block to 'feel' is muscles that are too tight. The tighter your muscles (particularly those in your arms) when you swing the club the less 'feel' (or control) you have over the movement. The more relaxed

they are the better you will feel what you are doing - up to a point. If you relax to a state of floppiness then your 'feel' diminishes again.

It takes time to develop 'feel'. You will have to hit 50, 100 or even 200 balls (preferably not in one session). But learning 'feel' is the only way to develop an efficient, consistent swing.

Set realistic goals

Don't try to play like a pro immediately – it's a recipe for disaster. Whether you like it or not, you have to start from your real standard. By all means have an ambitious target to aim for, but then break it down into little steps that are much more manageable. Each time you achieve one of these you can move on to the next one. This way you demonstrate your own success to yourself by moving on, and this breeds self confidence.

For example, if the longest drive you have ever hit is 200yd, trying to hit that distance off every tee is unrealistic, as that was your best ever drive. If you try to do that on each tee shot then you are more than likely to see yourself fail. However, if you instead attempt first

Concentration is the key to success. Here, Mary Beth Zimmerman is totally absorbed in assessing her putt.

to hit, say, 5 out of 10 drives 200yd; then the following week try to hit 8 out of 10 shots 200yd and so on; then reset the distance after a month and aim to hit just one shot 210yd, then 2 and so on upwards, you will see little successes which will lead to big successes.

Analyze and review your play accurately

Telling yourself that what you did is good or bad or right or wrong is mostly a waste of time. It doesn't tell you anything useful but worse than that, it tends to make you try too hard to do it right. (And the harder you try . . . !)

Your comments to yourself should be factual. They should be observations of what you actually did which will help you make the appropriate corrections. For example, 'I'm playing like a drain' tells you nothing. But 'I've dropped a lot of shots through slicing the ball on long shots' tells you a lot more about what you might need to correct.

You must beware, however, of substituting analysis for feel. Having analyzed what you did you then have to learn to 'feel' it.

Experiment and make errors

Be willing to change and try different ways of hitting the ball. There is no one way to do it. The suggestions in this book are guidelines which will allow you to develop and improve *your* way of playing.

Experimenting can be fun and a great way to increase your 'feel'. You can sometimes learn as much from 10 minutes doing things the wrong way as in an hour of doing them the right way. Try it and see.

Warming up before practice at a golf school. Learning golf in groups is becoming increasingly popular.

Patience

Learning, however much it is speeded up, takes time. It's often a case of two steps forward, one step backward. When you have a bad patch it's vital that you don't panic. If you are patient your form will return. If you are impatient you will find it difficult to concentrate, which will keep you playing badly. You will then lose confidence, and that will drag you into a 'slump'.

Even the best players lose their form sometimes. Be patient with yourself and yours will return much more quickly.

Applying these guidelines to your golf is like using the best oil, petrol and tyres in your car. Your car can do without the best but it won't give you the same performance. It's the same with your golf, so here they are again.

- Do one thing at a time
- Develop 'relaxed' concentration
- Concentrate on what you *are* doing
- Practise 'feel'
- Set realistic goals
- Analyze accurately
- Experiment
- Be patient

GOLF PHYSICS

CONTROL AND THE CLUBHEAD

Most of the tips you see in the golf magazines, and most of the guidelines that we offer in this book, have one purpose in mind; to help you control the way your clubhead strikes the ball so that the ball goes in the direction of your, rather than its, choosing. The only time you can influence the golf ball is when the clubface is in contact with it. (If you have managed to influence the direction and flight of a golf ball without the clubface being in contact we'd love to hear from you!)

In fact, if you obey a few basic fundamentals with your body and have the clubhead doing a few important things at impact your handicap will be on its way down. Understanding what is happening at impact can help you to help yourself where your golf is concerned, so in this chapter we will explore the governing principles involved.

There are four factors which determine the way the ball travels. They are the path of the clubhead, the angle at which the clubhead comes into the ball (ie steep or shallow), the alignment of the face of the club and the speed of the clubhead.

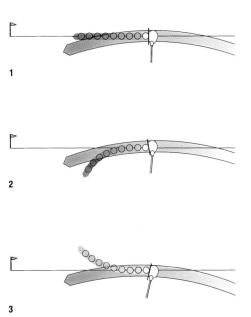

1

2

3

Three different paths of the clubhead at impact: *1*, with the path of the clubhead moving towards the target at impact the ball will start towards the target; *2*, with the path of the clubhead moving from out to in at impact the ball will start to the left of the target; and, *3*, with the clubhead moving from in to out at impact the ball will start to the right of the target.

The path of the clubhead

Your body is built in a way that ensures that you always swing the club along a curved path (you will see this from the diagrams). The path along which your clubhead is travelling as it strikes the ball determines in which direction the ball will start its journey.

In the illustrations below you will see what happens when you strike the ball with the clubhead travelling along three different paths at impact. In all three cases the face of the club is SQUARE (ie, at right angles) to the path of the clubhead.

In illustration 1, your clubhead is travelling directly towards the target at impact (ie, along the target line) and your clubface is square to the path of the clubhead. The result is that the ball starts off STRAIGHT towards the target.

In illustration 2, your clubhead is travelling to the LEFT of the target (ie, from out to in) and once again the clubface is square to the path of the clubhead. The result now is that the ball starts off to the LEFT of the target.

In illustration 3, your clubhead is travelling to the RIGHT of the target (ie, from in to out across the target line) and the clubface is again square to the path of the clubhead. The result is that the ball starts off to the RIGHT of the target.

The rule is: Provided the clubface is square to the path of the clubhead, the ball will start in the same direction that the clubhead is travelling at impact.

The angle of approach

The angle at which your club approaches the ball will determine the height that the ball will reach during its flight. A steep angle of approach means that your clubface will have less loft when it strikes the ball and the ball will therefore travel lower through the air. A shallow angle of approach means that your clubface will have more loft at impact and so the ball will travel along a steeper trajectory through the air.

The position of the ball in the stance will to a certain extent determine the angle of approach. If the ball is set back in the stance contact occurs earlier in the swing, and your clubface has less loft when it meets the ball,

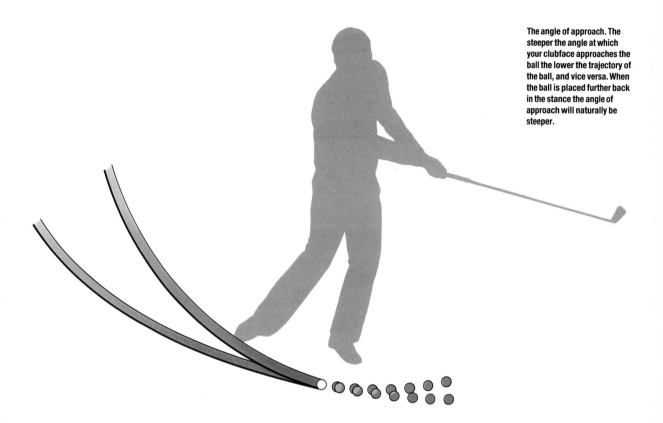

The angle of approach. The steeper the angle at which your clubface approaches the ball the lower the trajectory of the ball, and vice versa. When the ball is placed further back in the stance the angle of approach will naturally be steeper.

making the ball fly lower. If the ball is placed forward in the stance contact occurs later in the swing, and your clubface is more lofted when it reaches the ball thus making it fly higher. (See illustration above.)

Alignment of the clubface

Whether or not your clubface is square to the path of the clubhead at impact determines whether or not your ball will curve in flight. As you have already seen, when your clubhead meets the ball square to the clubhead path the ball will travel straight in the direction of the clubhead path (see p. 18).

When your clubface meets the ball facing CLOSED, ie, to the left of the clubhead path, the ball will curve to the left (p. 20, illustration 2).

When your clubface meets the ball facing OPEN, ie, to the right of the clubhead path, the ball will curve to the right as it travels (p. 20, illustration 3).

The ball curves because by meeting the ball with anything but a square clubface you are giving the ball a glancing blow and thereby

BRAIN STORM

"For the last few holes my equilibrium was sabotaged. I had to overcome it, but my fingertips were on fire. I was afraid the ball would explode like a grenade. I don't know why. The demons were haunting me and I had to exercise total, immediate amnesia, to stop the haemorrhaging."
– *Mac O'Grady, after winning the 1987 Tournament of Champions at La Costa, San Diego.*

GOLF PHYSICS

SPEED = DISTANCE

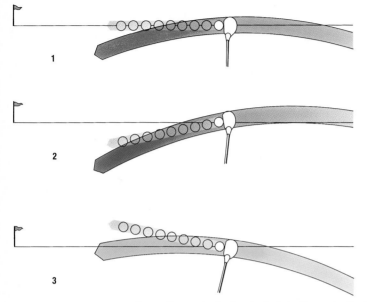

Above: The alignment of the clubface. These illustrations show how a similar swingpath with three different clubface alignments can produce three very different results: 1, straight; 2, hook; and, 3, slice.

Right: The position of the ball in the stance will affect the initial direction of the ball. The ball placed further back in the stance *(top)* is struck earlier in the swingpath while the clubhead is still travelling to the right of the target. The middle illustration shows the ideal position of the ball for this particular swingpath, where the ball is struck while the clubhead is travelling directly towards the target. The bottom illustration shows what happens when the ball is placed too far forwards and the clubhead is travelling left of the target.

correct your mistakes more accurately. The way the ball travels can give you vital clues as to what you did at impact.

To summarize, the four major factors to understand are:
- The path of the clubhead determines the direction in which the ball starts out.
- The angle of approach determines the height that the ball reaches.
- Clubhead alignment, combined with clubhead path, determines the amount of sidespin on the ball.
- Clubhead speed determines how far the ball travels.

Of course all of these factors interplay with each other. It is what makes golf interesting.

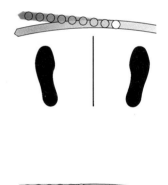

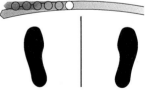

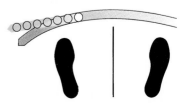

imparting spin to the ball. It is the spin that makes the ball curve.

Spin can be both a help and a hindrance. A little sidespin can help you curl the ball round obstacles. Too much sidespin and you curl the ball into the trees.

Those of you who have watched golf on TV will have seen the pros impart tremendous backspin on shots played to the greens, usually with short irons. The extra loft on these clubs, say from the 8 iron upwards, means they create spin much more easily than the straighter-faced clubs, which will tend to drive the ball more forwards and over.

Clubhead speed
The speed with which you swing the clubhead determines how far you will hit the ball.

The faster you swing your clubhead the further the ball will go for a given club, *provided* you maintain the same swing path, angle of approach, and clubhead alignment. Be aware, however, that there are limits to how fast you can swing the club – it depends on build, degree of control over the club and strength, although the latter has to be coupled with rhythm and timing.

Understanding how the way you use the club affects the flight of the ball can help you

Bernhard Langer at impact, displaying the strength and aggression that are a feature of his game.

THE GRIP

5

When you watch professional golfers playing or practising you will see them using swings that all look different in various ways – some fast, some slow, some flat, some steep and so on. Yet they all hit the ball solidly, accurately, and consistently, so there are some things about what they are doing that must have a common factor. This common factor is basic technique, which is explained in this chapter.

The information given here is not an exhaustive analysis of every little element involved in swinging a golf club. It contains simple instructions so that you do not fall into some of the traps described earlier in the book.

Many golfers become obsessed with doing things absolutely correctly, and then get confused when six different pros tell them six different things, all of them correct. What is important is that whatever you do gets the ball consistently close to your target. If you are achieving that, then making what you do as comfortable as possible is the next step.

Use the advice in this book, and particularly the next two chapters, as a basis for your game. Experiment with it, and adapt it to suit you as an individual.

The grip

Getting the grip right at the beginning can spare you endless hours of misdirected shots. The correct grip will enable you to swing the club through the ball with the clubhead square at impact, and feel comfortable.

The majority of golfers favour one of two types of grip, known as the overlap and interlock grips respectively (see illustrations).

In the case of the overlap or Vardon grip your left hand holds the end of the club about ½in from the top, and your right hand is placed just below the left with the little finger of your right hand overlapping the index finger of your left. As a very rough guide (it is rough because all our hands are shaped slightly differently), the V formed between your thumb and forefinger on each hand points towards your right shoulder.

The interlocking grip is used more by ladies than men. In this grip, instead of the little finger of your right hand overlapping the index finger on your left hand, it interlocks with it, hence the name. In both cases, the hands should fit together snugly on the club, the base of the right thumb on top of the left thumbnail.

Right: For the interlock grip, the little finger of the right hand interlocks with the index finger of the left hand.
Far right: The overlap grip, sometimes called the Vardon, is used by the majority of golfers. For this grip the little finger of the right hand overlaps the index finger of the left hand.

Seve Ballesteros
demonstrates an important
attribute that all of the world's
great golfers seem to possess
– a balanced follow through.

GRIP/POSTURE

A simple and quick way to find your grip is to first line up the bottom of the blade so that it is at right angles to the direction of the target line – that is, square to the direction you want the ball to go in (many golfers make the mistake of not looking at the bottom of the blade and end up with the clubface open or closed). Stand with the club in the middle of your stance and hold it first with your right hand, making sure the blade still points towards the target. Then just reach out and hold the club with your *left* hand as if you were shaking hands with someone. Then take your right hand off the club and replace it, again as if you were shaking hands. Doing the last part with your eyes closed can be useful as well.

The club needs to be held reasonably softly, but firmly enough to ensure that it does not slip in your hands.

Once you have checked your grip, beware of fiddling with it. When you have a new grip you will quite often be tempted to lift one or two fingers and make some adjustments to get comfortable. As you do this you are likely to turn your hand around the shaft, so altering the position of your grip, and therefore the clubface. Golfers are apt to describe a new grip as uncomfortable, when unfamiliar would be a more appropriate description; the most comfortable way of holding the club is likely to be what you are used to.

Sometimes you will hear a grip being described as either 'strong', or 'weak': 'strong' meaning the hands are turned more under the shaft, exposing the knuckles of the left hand and hiding those of the right, and 'weak' meaning the hands are turned over the shaft, showing more knuckles on the right hand and less on the left. If you look at players such as Bernhard Langer, who shows three knuckles on his left hand as he grips the club, and Jack Nicklaus, who shows only one, it will seem as if there is indeed no one way of gripping the club, as both these gentlemen are very proficient! The grip to suit you, however, lies almost certainly somewhere in between.

Remember that these are suggestions to guide you. You need to experiment and find the most comfortable way for you to bring the clubhead square to the ball at impact.

Stance, alignment and posture

In the address position you stand with your feet approximately shoulder width apart. If your feet are too close together it will be difficult to keep your balance, whereas if your feet are too far apart it will become more difficult to swing freely and move your weight.

If you were to draw a line joining up the toes of your shoes (the footline), it should be parallel to the target line. This means that sometimes it might look as if you are aiming left of the target. There are quite a number of good players who purposely aim slightly to the left of the target with their feet – for example, Mark James and Lee Trevino, who both play the ball from left to right as their stock shot very successfully indeed. This is much more common than a closed stance, which, while generally adopted by players who favour a draw (see page 54), tends to restrict freedom through impact.

Your weight should be evenly distributed on both feet, and your body should be as relaxed as possible without being sloppy. Your legs should be slightly flexed at the knees, your bottom sticking out slightly, your shoulders relaxed, and you should be breathing normally.

Ball position

For the majority of shots the ball should be positioned just inside your left heel, a comfortable distance away from you. This distance will vary, depending on which club you are using and your build. Shorter people usually position the ball further away from them, taller people place it closer. The important thing is to be able to get a free swing at the ball, from a solid base.

TRUSTY FRIEND

"I don't know a lot about swing technique. And I don't want to. I have a swing that I can trust. Lee Trevino once told me to keep it as long as it worked. That's something I've always remembered." – *Nancy Lopez, early in her career*

Far left: For good posture the weight is evenly balanced, the knees flexed and the body relaxed. The back is slightly arched to give a purposeful feel to the set up.
Left: In this example of poor posture, the shoulders are rounded, giving a weak base from which to start the swing.

There are some shots where you will want to position the ball further back in your stance. These include shorter shots where you will want more backspin, and punched shots.

The swing step by step

Although the golf swing has here been broken down into seven steps, it is important to bear in mind that it is actually one complete movement. The effect you are trying to achieve with your body and club is similar to that created when you crack a whip. Because the whip is flexible, the tip lags behind when you take your hand back. When you bring your hand forward the tip of the whip has not gone fully back yet, so it is going backwards even as the whip handle is going forwards. Then a point is reached when, because the tip is attached to the handle, it is forced to 'catch up'. It does so with tremendous speed. Your golf swing uses a similar principle to create the clubhead speed that sends the ball into the distance.

The illustrations on pp. 26-7 show the positions of the swing from both the side and behind. You do not have to 'do' most of these movements. They will happen naturally provided you stay relaxed and do not try too hard.

Address (1)

Your weight is evenly balanced between both feet with the ball positioned just inside your left heel. Your stance and posture are purposeful but relaxed and your foot line is parallel with, or slightly open to, the target line. You will no doubt have heard of the instruction 'keep your head down'. Beware of this as it can actually cause more problems, leading to your chin being too close to your chest and thus making your shoulder turn very restricted. 'Keep your head down' really means 'keep your eyes on the ball'.

Backswing (2)

Your backswing is started by moving the club in a relaxed fashion away from the ball on the inside of the target line, low to the ground. Your left shoulder will be moving across towards the middle of your stance at this stage. This is the start of the shoulder turn. When your club is roughly parallel to the ground – that is, the middle of your backswing – your left arm will be relatively straight and your right elbow will be starting to fold. A good check at this point is that your right elbow should not

BASICS I: THE SWING
SIDE VIEW/BACK VIEW

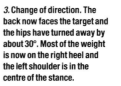

Two views of the swing
1. Address position. The weight should be evenly balanced and the foot line parallel to the target line. Posture should be purposeful.

2. Backswing. The club moves back inside the target line, the shoulders start to turn, the left arm remains straight while the right elbow starts to fold towards the left elbow.

3. Change of direction. The back now faces the target and the hips have turned away by about 30°. Most of the weight is now on the right heel and the left shoulder is in the centre of the stance.

4. Downswing. The hands and arms retrace the path of the backswing, and the body weight transfers smoothly to the left side and the hips open.

5

6

7

5. Impact. 75 per cent of the weight is on the left heel. The hands are just in front of the ball, and the head still fractionally behind it.

6. Follow through. The right arm straightens as the clubhead overtakes the hands. The weight is moving to the outside of the left foot.

7. The finish. The club is taken over the left shoulder and the arms fold. The chest faces the target. The whole body remains well balanced despite 80 per cent of the weight being on the outside of the left foot.

DOWNSWING TO FINISH/RHYTHM AND TIMING

have drifted away from the left. If your elbows are the same distance apart as they were at address you are well on your way to a respectable action. As your shoulders turn their full extent you will notice your hips following suit, but not to the same degree.

Change of direction (3)

As you can see, turning your shoulders away so that your back faces the target shifts your weight over to your right heel. At the top of your backswing your weight will be as much as 75 per cent on the right side. Your back will now be facing the target and your left shoulder will be in the centre of your stance. Your backswing and downswing are connected by the change of direction, which should be flowing in order to maintain the rhythm of the swing.

The backswing becomes the downswing when your hands and arms move down towards the ball. You start this movement just before your club has stopped moving backwards so that you create a 'lag', which begins the whip effect described earlier. At the same time your weight will start to move towards your left heel.

Downswing (4)

Your hands and arms are now well on their way to the ball, retracing the path of the backswing. The clubhead is lagging well behind but, helped by the flexibility of the shaft, picking up speed rapidly. Your weight is moving smoothly towards your left side and your hips are opening towards the target.

Impact (5)

At impact your weight is 75 per cent on your left heel and your hands are just in front of the ball. The momentum of the clubhead will pull

your right shoulder under your chin, enabling your hips to open freely.

Follow through (6)

Your right arm now starts to straighten as it is pulled through by the speed of the clubhead, which has now gained sufficient impetus to overtake the hands for the first time. The momentum of the clubhead should pull your weight over to the outside of your left foot.

The finish (7)

As the clubhead loses speed, both arms start to fold at the elbow and the club goes over the left shoulder to the finish. Your chest is now facing the target, with your weight almost completely on the outside of your left foot. Swinging to a balanced finish like this is another of the common denominators between good players. Very seldom will you see a professional lose his balance at the finish.

Summing up

Again, there are no hard and fast rules about the golf swing. It is a movement open to all kinds of interpretation. If you can keep your centre of gravity reasonably still, and swing your arms and hands in a roughly semi-circular fashion around you, you have all it takes to hit the ball reasonably well.

Rhythm, timing and trying too hard

Watch children learning a golf swing. They are not very interested in analysis of the swing, they just enjoy hitting the golf ball. They imitate what they see and try out different things, very rapidly learning how to make the appropriate movements.

This ability to learn movement is in all of us but becomes less effective when we try too hard. Beginners try too hard to just hit the ball or to hit it up in the air. Others try too hard to hit the ball a long way, and almost everyone – professionals included – tries to hit the ball perfectly. The problem with trying too hard is that your muscles become tense, making your movements stiff and jerky. In fact, the harder you try to make the correct swing the more difficult it will be for you to do so. Trying too hard tenses your muscles so much you cannot get your body into the right position.

Rhythm and timing improve when you cease using too much effort. You have to

THAT SWEET FEELING

"One of the greatest pleasures in golf is the sensation a golfer experiences at the instant he contacts the ball flush and correctly. He always knows when he does for then and only then does a distinctive 'sweet feeling' sweep straight up the shaft from the clubhead and surge through his arms and his whole frame." – *Ben Hogan*

Laura Davies seems to be the exception that proves the rule (see photograph on p. 23)! She is shown here in a very unorthodox follow through position. The longest hitter in the women's game, she is living proof that there's no one way of hitting a golf ball.

'feel' rhythm, and some people are able to do this better than others. Perhaps that is a part of what makes champions. Everyone has a slightly different rhythm to their swing and, as usual, there is no one right way.

In your bid to hit the ball it is quite likely that you will either breathe shallowly or hold your breath. As well as not being ideal for your health, it can also affect your rhythm. You may find it beneficial to breathe out as you make your downswing and follow through, particu-larly on shots that you think are difficult. Your breath should come out smoothly and evenly. If it comes out in a rush or after you have struck the ball, you are using too much effort.

You probably swing quite effortlessly when you take a practice swing without a ball. Use your practice swing to get a 'feel' for how much effort you need to use to hit the ball.

Alternatively, however much effort you think you need to use in order to hit the ball, halve it. You will always over-estimate.

BASICS II: THE SHORT GAME
USING DIFFERENT CLUBS

6

The last chapter covered the parts of your technique that will stay the same most of the time, no matter what club you are using. This chapter introduces you to some of the variations that are necessary when you use different clubs. Although they vary according to the club, they are still fundamental to developing a sound, repeatable technique.

The clubs
The parts of your swing that have already been described do not need to be modified for any particular golf club, as long as you are attempting a reasonably full shot. All that will change is the distance that you stand from the ball, and therefore your swingplane. Obviously, the longer the club the further away you stand from the ball, and the flatter your swingplane will tend to become.

With the short irons (ie, 8, 9, pitching and sand wedges), your swingplane will be at its steepest, thus delivering more of a downward blow and imparting more backspin. By moving the ball back in your stance, this effect is enhanced, as the ball is struck slightly earlier

in the downswing. This will also tend to make you take a deeper divot than when using a longer iron, as the club is travelling steeply downwards, even after impact. Please do not forget to put your divots back!

With the fairway woods you do not want to take much of a divot if at all possible, so it is best to play these shots with the ball no further back than just inside the left heel at address to ensure that the ball is struck at the very bottom of your downswing.

With the driver, however, you have the opportunity to play the ball from a tee, which makes it one of the most appealing shots to practise. Perched up in the air, it looks as if it will be easy to smash into the distance. A word of warning, however. If you spend more time practising your short game than you do with long irons and woods, you stand a much better chance of rapidly becoming proficient at the game. Time and time again, the temptation of being able to hit the ball as far as possible lures unwary golfers away from the far more valuable pastime of learning how to get the ball into the hole.

The type of club you use for a particular shot will determine the distance you stand from the ball and therefore your swingplane. The shortest distance will be with the wedge (below left), the longest with the driver (right), while the distance with the iron (middle) is between the two.

One of the greatest players of all time, Tom Watson was the world's foremost exponent of the short game in his heyday from the mid 1970s to the mid 1980s. His short game was played with a confidence and aggression that made it a consistent match winner.

BASICS II: THE SHORT GAME

PUTTING/THE GRIP

The overlap grip, which is the usual one for putting *(right)*. Two variations are the forefinger *(middle)*, when the forefinger of the right hand is extended down the grip, and the crosshands *(far right)*, made popular by Bernhard Langer.

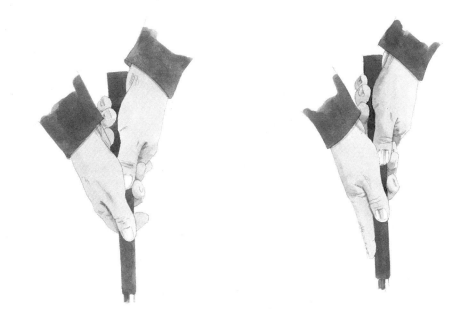

Putting

This is the single most important part of the game. If a professional golfer has shot a round of 70, he is likely to have used his putter more than twice as often as any other club in his bag. It is the department of the game where scores are made and money is won or lost. In terms of technique it is also the most diverse and interesting part of the game, and the most frustrating!

Watching the professionals, you will see all kinds of approaches. Some are hunched over the ball with their face only 3ft away from it, others have a very upright stance. Some golfers use the grips described earlier, others separate their hands on the club by anything up to a foot. In fact, the only thing that outdoes the variety of approaches to putting is the putters themselves. You have probably discovered all kinds of shapes and sizes of putter heads, and sometimes you will find that the grips have been altered to suit a particular individual.

Putting is about 'feel' more than any other shot in the game. To putt well you need to be able to judge the speed with which you will need to hit the ball so as to either get it in the hole or, if you miss, leave it as close as possi-

ble. You also have to judge the slope of the green so that you can estimate the effect it will have on the path of the ball as it travels towards the hole.

Let's approach putting as we did the swing, look at the basics first and see what the majority of good putters do.

The grip

The most common type of putting grip is the overlap grip described on page 22. It is easier to grip a putter comfortably, as most of the grips have a flat surface on top where your left thumb will be. This flat side is at right angles to the direction in which the blade is pointing, and will enable you to position your hands much more easily (see illustration).

It has now become quite common to see a crosshanded grip (see illustration), which has been made popular by Bernhard Langer. For this grip the position of your hands is reversed – that is, your right hand is at the top of the grip and your left hand is below your right hand.

You will also find many variations on these grips. For example, you may see the forefinger of one or both hands extended down the shaft. As always, try them out and see if you like them.

this 'feel', try hitting a dozen balls around the practice putting green to different holes, reading each putt before you hit it. Try to pick out the individual slopes on the green that make the ball break the way it does. You will soon notice that the ball will break more on a downhill sideslope than on a similar uphill sideslope. On a given 10ft putt, there may be 6in of break from right to left, provided you strike the ball just firmly enough to reach the hole. However, by hitting the ball firmly enough to go 18in past the hole, you may find that you only need to aim 3in to the right. In other words, the line that you choose depends on the speed that you intend to hit the ball. The harder you hit the putt, the less it will break.

Plumblining

Perhaps you may have seen the pros (or even your playing partner) performing an odd-looking ritual on the greens which involves hanging the putter vertically in front of their faces and squinting down the line. This is called plumblining, and it can be very useful for lining up putts which are difficult to read. If it is to be effective it must be used correctly, otherwise it can be misleading.

Posture, stance and ball position
Position the ball just inside your left foot with your feet fairly close together and your eyes over the ball. Because putting is a much softer, slower shot than any other, you do not have to generate a lot of power. This means that you do not need to use your body very much and can therefore take a 'quieter', less dynamic posture. Your body needs to be as relaxed as possible to aid smooth movement. Line yourself up so that when the blade of the club is immediately behind the ball, it faces in the direction you want the ball to travel in.

Although you hardly need to move your body, do not 'try' to keep it from moving. Instead, just allow your hands and arms to move the club back and then through. Your stroke should be smooth and effortless with no sudden movements, and the club should stop wherever it feels most comfortable.

Reading greens

The slopes on most greens are fairly obvious and reading them soon becomes relatively simple once you have had some experience in observing how much the ball breaks towards the hole on varying degrees of slope. Again, it soon becomes a matter of 'feel'. To develop

The posture for putting should be relaxed and 'quiet'.

BASICS II: THE SHORT GAME

PLUMBLINING

First, take up a shoulder-width stance facing the hole, directly on a line running from the centre of the hole, through the centre of the ball. Closing one eye, hold the putter grip between finger and thumb and suspend it in front of your eye so that either edge of the shaft runs through the centre of the ball. Make sure that the toe of the putter points to the hole. Holding the putter as still as possible, follow the edge of the shaft that runs through the centre of the ball upwards to a point level with the hole. Whichever side of the hole the

shaft now hangs is the side that the ball will break from. All you have to do now is judge the speed!

Chipping

There are three basic methods of chipping the ball, which are:

The chip and run

You normally play the chip and run with a 6, 7 or 8 iron when there are no obstacles such as bunkers, humps or hollows between the ball and the hole. You play the ball from a position towards the back of your stance, with the weight 60/40 in favour of the left side. You may find that a slightly open stance will be more comfortable here, as it allows you more freedom in the follow through area. Your shoulder stance will look narrower than usual as you do not need very much backswing for this shot.

Your backswing should be slightly in to out to produce the topspin needed to make the ball run. Your legs should stay reasonably still and relaxed during the backswing and your hips should open gently as you swing through impact to face the hole. You take the clubhead away from the ball low and slowly, only as far as the shot requires. Again, similar to putting, this is a 'feel' shot, which you will need to practise before you can judge length with accuracy. Keep the pace of this short swing as smooth and even as possible. Any hurried or jerky move can ruin not only the result, but your sense of where the clubhead is throughout the swing, which is all important for developing your sense of 'feel'.

The pitch

You would play a pitch shot from further away from the green than a chip and run, using a 9 iron or a pitching wedge. You can, however, play it instead of the chip and run, depending

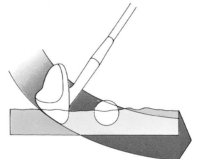

Left: The angle of the clubface necessary for a bunker shot when the ball is sitting virtually on the surface *(top)*, and when you have a plugged lie *(middle)*.
Below: The ideal position of the body for a simple sand shot. The stance is open, the clubface square to the target (although open in relation to the stance), allowing plenty of room for the slightly out to in swing needed for this shot.

BAD DAY AT THE OFFICE

Arnold Palmer, on one occasion when things were not going well on the greens or the fairways: "No worries, whatever happens I can always dig ditches for a living!"

BASICS II: THE SHORT GAME

SAND SHOTS

The short game is even more difficult when you're cold and wet! A miserable Ray Floyd, kitted out in a full set of waterproofs and looking for all the world like a frozen Bill Haley, chips to one of the more exposed greens at Turnberry, July 1986.

on which shot you find easier to play. It is really a miniature golf swing, played with the ball set back in your stance to help produce more backspin. Again, it will take some practice for you to get a real 'feel' for how far the ball will fly and roll.

The lob

This is played when you want extra height on the ball, either to stop the ball quickly or to clear an object such as a tree or high bank directly in front of you. The sand iron, being the most lofted club, is the best one to use, although the lob can be played with the wedge or 9 iron if you want more distance. This shot is played from just forward of the middle of an open stance, and with a slightly open clubface. In contrast to the low chip and run, you play the high lob with an out to in swingpath. One thing to guard against in this shot is the danger of the clubhead overtaking the hands before impact. This can lead to a bad contact with the ball (see the illustrations on p. 61), so keep the pace of the swing slow and even, letting the loft of the clubface do the work for you, rather than trying to force the ball into the air by rushing and forcing the club in early.

Bunkers

These are the source of a lot of unnecessary fear and frustration for many club golfer – unnecessary because with a little understanding of how the sand cushions the impact, you will find it easy to splash the ball out of the bunker, provided your lie in the sand is not too disastrous.

You play the bunker shot by striking the sand just behind the ball, as shown in the illustration on p. 35. As your club moves towards the ball it scoops a thin layer of sand between the ball and the clubface, cushioning the impact. The loft of the club lifts the ball out of the sand.

The technique is similar to that of the lob shot. Once again the stance is open, although this time more so. Making sure that your feet are well anchored in the sand, address the ball by holding the slightly open clubface directly above the spot on the sand you wish to strike, which should be 2-3in behind the

ball. Take the club slowly away a little outside the target line and, keeping an even pace, strike this spot on the sand, keeping the club moving forward and through to a full finish. By keeping the clubhead moving evenly like this, you can greatly reduce your chances of playing a bad shot. Gary Player, who is probably the greatest bunker shot player of all time, aptly described it as 'keeping the motor running'.

The most common cause of not getting out of a bunker first time is losing clubhead speed. It usually stems from fear – being afraid of hitting the ball too far. Remember that the sand takes all the speed out of the ball so you need to take this into account when you calculate each shot.

Beware of grounding your club (see page 46) in a bunker as you will be penalized for doing this.

Plugged lies

If your ball is buried in the sand the shot obviously becomes much more difficult. In this case you need a steeper angle of attack, so the shot will be played from much further back in your stance. Close the clubface and aim at a point about 1½in behind the ball, again holding the clubhead over the spot you wish to strike. Hit down and through this spot, and you will find that the ball will pop up and out of the bunker. It is difficult to gain any real height with this shot, so be careful if there is a high lip on the bunker. In this case it may be advisable to play out sideways, rather than going straight for the hole. A ball in a plugged lie is nearly always very difficult to get near the hole, so if you get down in 3 shots from this situation you will have done well (see illustration on p. 35).

SHORT FRIGHT

"I once shot a wild, charging elephant in Africa and it kept coming at me until dropping to the ground at my feet. I wasn't scared a bit. It would take a four-foot putt to really scare me to death!" – *Sam Snead*

PRACTICE

WARMING UP

Ask any golfer what they would want if they could be granted one wish for their golf, and their reply will most often be 'I wish I could be more consistent in my game.' Consistency of strike and scoring is what every golfer strives for, and that applies just as much to professionals as amateurs. Golf, like many sports, is a game of minimizing errors, and reducing the effects of the errors that you do make.

Developing this kind of consistency requires practice – lots of it. The practice, though, has to be of the right kind. You will have heard the expression 'Practice makes perfect', but this adage does not quite tell the whole story. What practice does is make permanent. Only perfect practice will make perfect. In other words, whatever you practise, both in attitude and technique, becomes permanent or 'grooved'. In fact, do anything over and over again and you will improve.

Many golfers are experts on the practice ground. They have put in many hours of practice and become very good at hitting golf balls one after the other from the same lie with the same club. However, when they get on the golf course where they have a different lie and a different club each time they find that they do not hit the ball as well. These golfers have become very good at what they practise – that is, hitting the ball from the same spot each time. But they have not practised hitting from different lies with different clubs and consequently are not as good when they get out on the golf course.

Practice is the golf laboratory. This is where you refine your game so that it is ready for the outside world. If you are thorough enough with your practice you will reap the rewards. This chapter will explore how to make practice more effective.

The warm up

It is quite widely recognized that by not warming up and stretching your muscles properly prior to exercise you run the risk of physically injuring yourself. What is less widely acknowledged is that you run the risk of 'mentally' injuring yourself also.

When you try to hit the ball with stiff muscles and joints it is much more difficult to find

rhythm and timing. You are highly likely to make some errors in your first few shots. When you make some errors at the very beginning you will probably say to yourself 'I'm not playing very well today'. You will try harder, tighten up, make errors, and eventually form a poor opinion of yourself as a golfer.

When you do the following series of exercises it is very important that you start gently and *do not force your body*. You should stretch only as far as is easy and comfortable. You should not 'bounce' into the extreme positions, or become breathless as you do them.

Arm swinging (see illustration)
This will loosen up your arms and shoulders. First put your right arm in the air and, keeping it straight, gently swing it in a circle at the side of your body. Repeat the movement 10 times. Then do the same with your left arm. Next reverse the direction and repeat with each arm. Lastly, do the same again with both arms simultaneously.

Twisting (see illustration)
This is to loosen up your hips, waist, and upper body. Hold one of your clubs behind your back by hooking the crook of your elbows around the shaft. The club will be held above your waist. With your feet about shoulder-width apart, turn as far as you comfortably can to the right, without forcing, and hold for a count of 10. Then turn as far as you can to your left, again without forcing, and hold for 10 seconds. Repeat exercise in each direction three times.

Waist bend (see illustration)
This will stretch your hamstrings. Place your hands on your hips and bend forward from your waist, keeping your back slightly arched, and hold for 2-3 seconds. Repeat this two or three times, but do not 'bounce' into position.

Club swinging
Hold two clubs together (say, a 5 and 6 iron) at the *same* time and take a few gentle practice swings. When you have followed through, make a reverse swing to bring the club back (as if you were going to hit a ball backwards). Besides loosening the muscles, some people find that this makes swinging one club that much easier. Make 10 to 12 swings as smoothly as you can.

Club selection

One of the skills required to play good golf is to select the appropriate club for the occasion. It is also a skill you will still be practising when you win your first open tournament!

When you go to a golf range you will see that the distances are usually indicated in bold letters on marker boards that are positioned at regular intervals. Unfortunately many golfers' practice seems to be composed of trying to hit the ball as far as possible with each club and using the marker boards to tell themselves how they are doing – a waste of practice.

You should use the marker boards to tell you how far you hit the ball the majority of the time with a given club. When you get out on the course, you will then know which club to use once you have estimated the distance you have to hit the ball. You can also use the range markers to help you to gauge distance accurately. Take a good look at what the distance of, say, 150yd *really* looks like. The more of this you do the more accurately you will select your clubs.

Some beginners and high handicap players spend so much time trying to work out which club they should use that they actually make the shot much more difficult. They dither so

Far left: Twisting
Middle: Waist bend
Left: Arm swinging

much as to whether or not they have the correct club that they lose their concentration and hit a bad shot, missing their target by more than the difference between the clubs over which they were puzzling.

Once you have decided which club you are going to use, trust your decision and stick to that club. Do not change your mind halfway.

A little and often

For most people a week's practice is better divided up into an hour each day, rather than one 3-hour and one 4-hour practice session. Whatever you are practising takes time to 'settle' into your system and the breaks in your practice are almost as important as the practice itself.

Of course, for most amateurs it is not practical to get out on the practice ground each day. However, you can put your garden to good use for practising your chip shots (and others if you have a larger garden!) and your living room carpet can be wonderful for practising your putting.

Practise awareness

It is very important to get the correct path for your clubhead, and control of the club comes from awareness or 'feel'. Make a point of practising awareness each time you practise and you will improve two things at the same time; one is your 'feel' for what you are doing, and the other is your concentration.

A great way to improve your putting 'feel' is to putt 40-50 balls with your eyes closed. You will 'feel' much more when you do not look.

Targets

Targets are a great way to make practice more interesting. Trying to land your ball as close as you can to a target is a good way to keep practice interesting. It adds a little pressure to the situation. However, don't make the target your main aim, especially if you are working on your mechanics. In putting, for example, you would probably use the hole as your target. An alternative would be to putt the ball towards the edge of the putting green and see how close to the edge you can make the ball stop. It is a great way to help yourself

The practice ground is the best place to listen to pros chatting or to watch them working at their game. All pros warm up by practising shortly before they go out to play. It is an essential part of every pro's routine.

LIES/ON THE COURSE

judge how hard or softly you need to hit the ball.

For chipping or short pitches you might stand an umbrella upside down on the ground and see how many balls you can land inside it. To add further pressure, you could see how many out of 10 you can get into the umbrella and then try to up your score out of 10 each time – but remember some of the pitfalls of goal setting (see page 14).

Placing the target quite close to you is a way to force you to hit short gentle shots, another way to increase your 'feel'. Even if you are practising tee shots, using the driver to hit the ball 40yd will teach you a lot about controlling the clubhead.

For your longer clubs your targets obviously should be larger areas. Control over the direction of the ball is what you are looking for when you use these clubs, rather than precise control of length.

Use different lies

When you play golf virtually every shot is different in the sense that it is played off a different lie every time. You very rarely use the same club twice in a row (except your putter), and the wind can be coming from different angles on each shot.

It is important to spend some time hitting shots from the same lie with the same club. This is how we groove what is called 'muscle memory'. It is also important to practise the skill of adapting to new lies and clubs, so when you are practising your putting, for instance, spread your practice balls out around the hole and make sure that you spend some time hitting balls from different lies in order

THE PRICE OF WINNING

"This is definitely the one to win for us girls – it's what I've been striving for since I took up the game. The thing that really made me nervous was the thought of giving a victory speech . . . you really need to practice for that!" – Laura Davies, after winning the 1986 British Women's Open at Royal Birkdale.

that you are forced to line up and read the green separately for each putt.

For longer shots, again spread your practice balls across an area so that you have to line up for each shot and try using a different club for every time.

If your practice ground is too crowded for you to do this or you practise at a golf range, at least take a different club for each shot. Imagine yourself playing a hole and try: first shot – driver; second shot – 5 iron; third shot – pitching wedge and so on.

Practising on the course

No, this does not mean that you should spread your practice balls out on the golf course! Making the transition between what you do on the practice ground and what you do on the course is sometimes a bit tricky. This is often because golfers try to make too big a step at one time.

For example, imagine Arthur, who has been learning how to draw the ball on the practice ground. He decides that it is now time to actually use his technique on the golf course. He is playing in a medal at the weekend, so he tries it out then. Arthur is a little nervous because he is playing in a competition, so he holds back a bit and does not hit the ball quite right. He thinks it is too risky to try his draw out now, and decides to try it again next week. Next week the same thing will happen again and he will continue to put it off until the following week.

What is happening is that Arthur is unwittingly leaving out several stages of practice essential to being effective on the golf course. He is taking too big a step.

So, if this were you, what should you do to make this transition from the practice ground to the golf course? Your first step ought to be to play a few rounds without trying to score well. This will give you a chance to get used to playing your draw (or whatever you have been practising) in the different perspective that the course creates. Your next step should be to try it out and try to score as well. Then use it in a friendly two ball and eventually, perhaps, in a medal. However, even in the medal you are using the competition as practice. You can

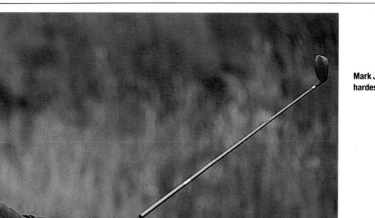

compete properly when you feel confident about using your draw in any situation.

Visualize what you are doing

Visualization is making mental pictures of whatever it is you are trying to do. The more detail you can create in your mental picture the more powerful the effect is likely to be. Research has shown that the effects of visualizing the swing you are trying to make can be almost as powerful as physically practising the swing itself. You can also use visualization to improve your self-image and, as a consequence, your confidence.

You have probably already sampled the effects of images on your play. If you have been watching good golfers for a while and then go out to play you strike the ball better for a short time. It is as if some of what the good golfers were doing has rubbed off on you. The effect usually disappears when you try to analyze what you were doing.

You can visualize before you play each shot or for 10 minutes each day sitting comfortably in a chair (or both). All you do is create a vivid detailed picture of yourself doing whatever it is you want to improve. If you want to develop a fade, for example, you might picture yourself at a particular hole where you would need that fade. You see yourself addressing the ball, you see and feel yourself swinging the club, you see the ball arcing from left to right and landing just where you aimed it.

As with all things, the more you visualize the better at it you will become.

Your short game

Many golfers put lots of practice into their swings at the expense of their short game. The importance of being good around the greens cannot be emphasized strongly enough. This is the area of the game where good scores are made or lost. Although you may find it more stimulating in the short term to whack the ball into the distance, you will find it more rewarding in the long term if you practise equal amounts of both your short and long game.

To summarize, the key points to be aware of when practising are:
● Warm up properly
● Discover how far you hit the ball with each club
● Practise a little and often
● Practise awareness
● Do not be too target conscious when practising a new technique
● Hit shots from different lies
● Practise on the course
● Visualize the shot before you hit it

GETTING ON THE COURSE

THE RULES

8

Many strokes are lost by amateurs through failure to understand the rules of the game. There are so many rules that even the professionals will occasionally lose shots by unintentionally breaking them. Besides those contained in the official rules of golf, there are local rules individual to each golf course. These take into account local conditions and are usually listed on the scorecard (see p. 49 for a typical example).

The complete rules of golf are not laid down here – that is a separate book in itself, which you are strongly recommended to read! Instead, there is a description of some of the most common things that happen on the golf course and which require the application of certain rules, as well as an outline of the basic etiquette of the game, which is neglected by some golfers and unfortunately affects others on the course.

Rules, etiquette and scoring are quite complex in this game. The rules are made and interpreted by the Royal and Ancient Golf Club of St Andrews, known as the R & A. It is not uncommon for a situation to arise in a competition that cannot be decided on there and then nor later by the committee. In these situations the R & A may be asked for an interpretation of the rules as they apply to the particular situation.

When in doubt, seek the advice of your club professional and do carry a rule book with you.

Those of you who have just started playing the game will also need to learn the different types of scoring systems too. But first, let's look at some of the rules.

Losing your ball

When you hit your ball, be it from the tee, fairway or green you are allowed 5 minutes to try to find it. If you cannot recover it in this time you must go back to the place from which you struck the lost ball and play another ball from there. To do this you drop the ball from shoulder height and as near as possible to the spot (tee shots can be replaced on a tee peg). You must count both shots in your score *and* add an extra shot as a penalty; stroke and distance. For example, if you hit the ball from the

tee and lose it in the rough, you must go back to the tee and play another ball. You have now played three shots, the two you struck and one penalty shot.

Out of bounds

The boundaries of the course are marked by white stakes, walls, fences or hedges; they will also be described in the local rules. If you hit a ball so that it finishes out of bounds the penalty is the same as if you had lost your ball – that is, stroke and distance.

Ball unplayable

Occasionally you will hit the ball into a position which makes it impossible to hit, although Bernhard Langer might dispute that (see photograph on p. 45). The rules give you three choices in this instance.

1. You can play the ball from the same position as your last shot and take a one shot penalty (again, stroke and distance).
2. You can drop the ball, moving back away from the hole as far as you like *provided* you keep the point at which you found your ball between you and the hole. The penalty is again one stroke.
3. You can drop the ball within two club lengths of where you found your ball, but not nearer the hole. Again, this will cost you a one stroke penalty.

Air shots

If you swing at the ball and miss for whatever reason, whether a dog barks or your trousers fall down, the stroke counts! Air shots are most likely to happen when you are trying to hit a ball that is buried in deep rough. The grass is sometimes so thick that it can stop your club and prevent it from making contact with the ball.

Water

Water on a golf course can be divided into two types: casual water and water hazards. *Casual water* is water that is not normally on the course; for example, puddles formed by bad weather. You can obtain relief (meaning that you can move your ball) in three circumstances:

1. If your ball lies in the water.

2. If you have to stand in the water in order to play it.

3. If your ball is on the green and there is water between it and the hole.

You obtain relief by dropping the ball within one club length of the nearest point at which none of the above conditions applies, provided it is not nearer the hole. On the green the ball is placed, rather than dropped, *at* the nearest point of relief *not within one club length*. If when you drop the ball it rolls more than two club lengths from where it landed or finishes nearer the hole, you have to drop it again. You must also re-drop if the ball rolls back into the casual water or if you have to stand in it to play the shot.

Water hazards are divided into two categories. These are lateral hazards, which are defined by red lines or red stakes, and water hazards (yellow lines or yellow stakes). Lateral hazards usually run roughly parallel to the direction of the hole.

If your ball lands in a water hazard, you have three options. You can either play the ball as it lies if this is possible (without grounding your club of course!) or drop the ball as far back as you like, keeping the point where the ball last entered the hazard between you and the hole. Failing this, you may drop the ball as near as possible to the spot where you played your last shot. If this shot was played from the teeing ground, the ball may be re-teed.

With a lateral hazard, you have all three of the above options, with the choice of two more. You can drop the ball within two club lengths of the point level with where the ball last entered, on *either* side of the hazard not nearer the hole. The penalty for dropping out of any water hazard is one stroke.

Ground under repair

Ground under repair is usually indicated by a white line around the relevant area or by prior warning posted on the club noticeboard. If your ball lies on ground under repair (G.U.R.)

Bernhard Langer proving the wisdom of the rule that makes it the sole responsibility of the player to judge whether or not a ball is playable; Panasonic European Open, Sunningdale, 1985.

GETTING ON THE COURSE

THE RULES

Mark Gardiner, Ian Woosnam's caddy, at the 10th green at the Belfry, playing one of the shots we haven't attempted to explain in this book! Ryder Cup, 1985.

you apply the same procedure as for casual water. You are not compelled to take relief from G.U.R. unless play is specifically prohibited by a local rule.

Moving a stationary ball
If a stationary ball is moved by the ball of another player, it must be placed exactly where it originally lay. If the exact spot cannot be found, the ball must be dropped or, on the putting green, placed as near as possible to its original point. The other ball must be played from where it lies.

Marking your ball
You may mark your ball on the greens. You must replace your ball in *exactly* the same position or you incur a two stroke penalty.

Mark the ball directly behind it using a ball marker or other small, flat object.

Flag in or out
If when putting from on the green your ball hits the flag you will be penalized two shots. You can putt from off the green and hit the flag with no penalty. If you wish to use the flag as a 'sighter', have one of your partners tend the flag while you putt, removing it immediately you strike the ball.

Grounding your club
When your ball lies in a hazard you are not allowed to touch the ground (or water when in a water hazard) with your club before completing your backswing. The penalty for grounding your club, as it is known, is two

strokes, or loss of the hole in match play.

These then are some of the most common rules you will encounter, but, as already stated, there are many rules to this game and you should really acquaint yourself with the full version (at least once).

Etiquette

Although there is no penalty for breaking golf etiquette, observing it possibly does more to make playing alongside other golfers pleasurable than anything else in the whole game.

Some of the 'rules' of etiquette will seem terribly obvious from the beginning. Others will become clearer the more you play. If you are just starting the game etiquette is easily forgotten while you try to remember all the other things you have to do.

Some of you will have had brushes with the 'etiquette police'. There are some of these at most clubs. They leap out at you when you least expect it and inform you, in a voice that carries all the way back to the clubhouse, that 'We don't do that sort of thing here', seemingly intent on making you as embarrassed as possible. Of course there are also the 'etiquette samaritans' who will give you the same information with a smile and without telling the whole world.

So let's look at some golfing do's and don'ts that will spare your blushes.

Taking care of the course

This element of etiquette is unfortunately much neglected. There are three areas where you are likely to affect the course so that it needs attention:

1. When your ball pitches on the green the force of the impact will cause a depression in the surface of the green (unless it is very hard). A ball putted over this depression will be deflected off its path. When you arrive at the green you should find your pitch mark and gently raise the turf with a pitch mark repairer or tee peg, so that the surface is level again.

2. On the fairway you will sometimes take a divot (see illustration on p. 61). A ball coming to rest in the divot mark is more difficult to play because of the 'tight' lie. Once you have played your shot and seen where your ball has

landed, you should retrieve your divot, replace it in the divot mark and press it down before moving on to play the next shot.

3. If your ball lands in a bunker you will leave footprints in the sand when walking in and out, and when you play the ball you will disturb the sand with your club. Any marks you make in a bunker should be smoothed over before you move on to your next shot.

Whenever you are on the green take care not to cause damage by placing your bag down carelessly or by dropping the flag on the green when you remove it from the hole. Leaning on your putter will also mark the green.

Your fellow players

When someone else is about to play a ball you should not move, or talk, or stand close to them. If you are on the putting green you should also make sure that you and/or your bag is not in line with the hole as someone is attempting to putt.

If you lose your ball you should allow the players behind you to play on as soon as you realize it will take some time to find it. You are not entitled to make other players wait the 5 minutes you are allowed before you incur a penalty.

Before you play your shot make sure that the players in front of you are well out of range. Being struck by a golf ball is a very painful experience and can be extremely dangerous.

Last but not least, a couple of hints for when you are on the green. First, take care not to walk directly on the line between another player's ball and the hole. The marks your spikes make can be enough to nudge the ball off course. Secondly, leave the green immediately you have played out the hole so that

SCORING

the players behind you can play on without interruption.

Almost every golf course will insist on a standard of dress – for example, no T-shirts. Most of them will also insist on no jeans, and no sharing of golf clubs so every player must have a bag of clubs.

Most etiquette is consideration for others. If everyone extended to other golfers the same courtesy that they would like themselves, there would never be any problems.

Unless there are special notices to the contrary, a two ball (ie, two people playing together) has priority over any other type of game. This means that if you are playing in a three- or four-ball game you should take care not to hold up a two-ball game behind you.

The general rule, however, is just common sense. If the group behind you (no matter their number) is playing appreciably faster than you are, and there are clear holes in front of you, let them through! It will make the game more pleasant for both groups.

Match play and stroke play

Generally you will only see two formats of scoring when you watch the pros play – match play and stroke play. However, you will encounter many variations of these playing golf as an amateur. The most common ones are outlined here, but you are sure to encounter others the more you play.

In match play you play your opponent hole by hole. Whoever has played the fewest shots at a given hole wins that hole. When someone is more holes ahead than there are holes left to play, the match is over; eg, a player who is 3 holes up with only 2 holes to play wins. If after 18 holes you have each won the same number of holes, you move into a sudden death play off. You play more holes until one of you wins one, and that person therefore wins the whole match.

In stroke play the total number of strokes you played during the 18 holes is compared with the total of every other competitor. The player with the fewest number of shots wins. If there is a tie for the lowest score many clubs operate a countback system. The winner is the best total on the last 9 holes of the com-

petition. If there is still a tie then it is the last 6 holes and then the last 3 holes. The alternative is a play off as in match play.

Stroke play demands a higher level of consistency than match play. In theory you could take many more strokes in total than your opponent in a match play competition and still win. Whether you lose a hole by one shot or 20 makes no difference; you still only lose that one hole. In stroke play, of course, in taking 20 shots each one would count against you.

Par, standard scratch score and stroke index
The par of a hole is the number of strokes it would theoretically take a very good player or pro to get the ball in the hole. It is always assumed that there will be two putts in that number of shots. Par is set for each hole according to the length of the hole and is also different for men and ladies. For men the par is set by the length or yardage of the hole, whereas for ladies the yardage is used only as a guide for the par. For men a yardage of 250yd and under is a par 3, 250-476yd is a par 4 and 476yd and over is a par 5. For ladies, up to 200yd is par 3, 200-400yd is par 4 and over 400yd is par 5.

So when you hear that a professional is 3 under par in a tournament, it means that he has taken 3 strokes fewer than par. Standards are so high these days that it is not uncommon to see scores of 20 or more under par in good weather conditions at the end of a 4-round tournament.

The par for each hole is shown on the scorecard, as is the standard scratch score (S.S.S.). The S.S.S. may differ from the par depending on the total length and the difficulty of the course.

The S.S.S. is normally based on the yardage, except in cases where the terrain, size of greens, prevailing weather conditions, hazards etc. make the course unusual. When the S.S.S. is different it is usually by one or two less than par.

The stroke index of a hole (S.I.) is a ranking of the difficulty of that hole as compared with other holes on the course. The S.I. is used to decide on which holes you receive shots according to your handicap.

Handicaps

Golf is famous (or perhaps notorious) for its handicap system. The purpose of handicaps is to allow players who do not play so well to contest evenly with very good players (sometimes even professionals – hence the term Pro-Am). A handicap is an allowed number of strokes per round that can be subtracted from the total number of strokes taken to give a net score. In theory this score would be equal to that of a good player.

To obtain a handicap you have to be a member of a club affiliated to your area golf union, and submit three completed score cards from competitions you have played. An average of your scores is worked out and the S.S.S. of the course is subtracted from it. This gives you your handicap. The way your handicap changes depends on many factors, and you should consult your club officials for an in-depth explanation.

In stroke play you just subtract your handicap from your total score at the end of the round to obtain your net score. In match play, whichever player has the higher handicap receives ¾ of the difference between the respective handicaps (fractions are rounded up or down to the nearest whole number). You

A typical scorecard

SSS31   SSS31 TOTAL 62

COMPETITION:

PLAYER ....

DATE ....

HANDICAP ....

STROKES RECEIVED ....

MARKER ....

FIRST NINE

Marker's Score	Hole	Yards	Par	Stroke Index	Player's Score	Won x Lost – Half 0
	1	434	4	1		
	2	104	3	17		
	3	386	4	7		
	4	340	4	15		
	5	508	5	9		
	6	421	4	3		
	7	390	4	11		
	8	557	5	5		
	9	193	3	13		
	OUT	3333				

SECOND NINE

Marker's Score	Hole	Yards	Par	Stroke Index	Player's Score	Won x Lost – Half 0
	10	460	4	2		
	11	422	4	6		
	12	459	4	4		
	13	146	3	18		
	14	302	4	16		
	15	380	4	8		
	16	365	4	12		
	17	215	3	10		
	18	492	5	14		
	IN	3252				
	OUT	3333				
	TOTAL	6585				

Marker's Signature ....

Player's Signature ....

HANDICAP ....

NET SCORE ....

SCORING

then receive those strokes according to the stroke index.

The maximum handicap is 28 for men and 36 for ladies. As you improve and submit more cards your handicap will go down.

As with any system of rules, there are people who try to manipulate them for their own benefit. Sometimes you will discover players who, through careful manipulation of the rules, have managed to maintain a higher handicap than their play warrants. Less often you will meet players with a handicap that is lower than it should be because they enjoy the status of being a 'low' handicapper.

Two, three and four balls, foursomes and greensomes

Two, three and four balls refer to the number of balls in play and hence the number of people playing. A two ball is often called a single and can refer to match play or stroke play. A three ball is usually only used in stroke play competitions. A four ball also refers to match play or stroke play format. A four ball better-ball is a type of four ball in which you have teams of two playing against each other. Each team uses the best of its two scores at each hole to match against the best of the other team's two scores.

Foursomes again means that a team of two takes on another team of two. The players in each team use one ball and hit it alternately. They also take turns to hit off the tee irrespective of the score at the previous hole; ie, one player tees off on the odd numbered holes, the other on the even numbered.

A greensome is where each member of a team hits a ball off the tee. The ball in the best position is selected and they then hit that ball alternately.

Stableford

In a stableford you are allocated points on each hole according to how much under par you are after you have subtracted your handicap, ie, your net score. You receive 1 point if you score 1 over par at a given hole (known as a bogey), 2 points for a par, 3 points for 1 under par (known as a birdie), 4 points for 2 under par (known as an eagle), and 5 points for a 3 under par (known as an albatross and very rare). Whoever has the greatest number of points at the end of the competition wins.

A characteristic of stableford competitions is that, rather than penalize you for your bad play, they reward you for your good play – which is very encouraging.

The eclectic

An eclectic competition runs over a period of time. You take your best scores at each of the holes of your club course over the duration of the competition and add them together to produce a total. Your total, therefore, will include your scores at individual holes but from different occasions. At the end of the competition you have some idea of what you might score if you played your very best golf for 18 holes.

The Texas scramble

This is an interesting format for playing, particularly if you are playing with very good players or pros. All the players hit their tee shots. They select whichever ball lands in the best position and pick up all the others. Then everyone plays their own ball from the same place as the selected ball. If you play with a pro you will get some idea of the positions that professionals hit their shots from.

Handicaps can be used in all the competitions covered here (except a Texas scramble), but there are variations in how the handicaps are applied. Sometimes you will not be allowed your full handicap but a particular fraction instead depending on the type of competition and the committee.

BAD CASE OF THE YIPS

"The word got round that my putting was terrible. I had the yips. One guy asked me to putt everything – including the tiddlers – and I couldn't blame him. It wasn't fun. If I had carried on putting like that I would have had to call it a day sooner or later." – *Bernhard Langer, recalling a Hennessy Cup match in the 1970s.*

A troublefree path for Nick Faldo at St. Andrews, which probably has the widest fairway in the world and certainly one that it's impossible to miss from the tee at the 18th.

VARIATIONS

UPHILL/DOWNHILL LIES

The description of the swing in Chapter 5 assumed that you were playing off a normal lie and that you wanted to hit a straight shot. However, there are many instances in golf where you will have to hit the ball off a peculiar lie or will want to make the ball fly with a different trajectory (shaping the shot). This chapter is called Variations because it describes eight of the most common adaptations you might want or need to make your game as effective as possible, given the different conditions you are likely to encounter.

You may find some adaptations easier to make than others, a factor to be taken into account in your course management. Spending some time practising variations will not only add some variety to your shot-making but will also make your practice more interesting for you – a key element for concentration and learning.

Uphill lies

Sometimes your ball will end up in a position which means that you will be hitting the ball uphill. When you take your stance you will find your left foot is higher than your right foot, so obviously some modifications are needed (see illustration).

To play this shot you should stand with your weight back on your right foot and your shoulders as parallel as possible with the ground. It is quite likely that you will feel a little bit uncomfortable (or unfamiliar) but that is often the case when adapting to different conditions. Getting your shoulders parallel to the ground is very important. It allows you to produce a free swing and gets the clubface into the ball correctly. The shape and production of your swing are the same as those described in Chapter 5.

The ball will not travel as far as it would if you were hitting off a flat lie, and even less distance if the point at which the ball pitches is higher than you are. This means that you will have to allow for this when assessing which club to use. Typically, you will need to take one more club than you would if you were playing off a flat lie, although which one will, of course, vary according to the steepness of the lie.

Downhill lies

This time the ball is on a downslope, forcing you to hit it downhill. When you take your stance your right foot is now higher than your left foot, but the technique for hitting the ball is slightly different to the uphill lie.

Position yourself so that the ball is back in your stance. When you swing, allow your weight to go to the left side even if it means a slight walking after effect as you follow through (your natural tendency will be to shift your weight backwards to counter gravity pulling you down the hill). Keep the angle of your shoulders the *same as if you had a flat lie*. Keeping your shoulders parallel to the slope at address here will put too much weight on your left side.

The ball travels further when you hit it off a downhill lie. It lands even later in its trajectory if the point at which the ball pitches is lower than you are. Again you must allow for this extra distance in your clubbing. The ball will also travel lower through the air.

Below left: **For uphill lies the weight is back on the right foot and the shoulders are parallel with the ground. For downhill lies** *(right)* **the ball is positioned back in the stance, but the shoulders are the same as for a flat lie.**

Far left: For a sideways uphill lie, the ball is higher than the feet. The grip is shortened and the posture is more erect.
Left: For a sideways downhill lie the ball is lower than the feet, the knees are flexed and the ball is slightly closer to the body.

Sideways lies

When the ball lands on a hill that slopes sideways in front of you (ie, left to right or right to left as you look at the hole) it will be higher or lower than your feet when you address it. Again, some alterations to your stance will be necessary in order to hit the ball properly.

Ball lower than feet

When the ball is lower than your feet you will have to find a way to get your clubhead down to the level of the ball. You do this by flexing your knees more than usual until the clubhead is low enough to meet the ball squarely without any danger of topping it (see illustration). If you normally grip the club short (ie, slightly down the grip), you could, in addition to flexing your knees, grip the club closer to the top. You will also need to stand slightly closer to the ball.

The effect of all this is that your swingplane becomes steeper and your clubhead will be moving from out to in at impact. The ball may fade from left to right as it travels towards the target, so you need to allow for this when you address the ball by aiming left of the target.

Ball higher than feet

When the ball is higher than your feet you must shorten your grip to compensate for this. You should also 'stand tall' to make sure that you have plenty of room in which to swing the club (see illustration).

Your swingplane will be shallower on this kind of lie, producing a more in to out clubhead path. The ball may draw from right to left as it travels towards the target. To allow for this, aim the ball right of the target at address.

The shortening of your grip for a ball higher than your feet and the flexing of your knees for a ball lower than your feet are both to help you keep your swingplane as close to its normal position as possible. You probably will not get it to be exactly the same, but the closer the better.

Fading the ball

Fading the ball means hitting it in a way that makes it move from left to right as it goes towards the target (see illustration). You will remember from Chapter 4: Golf Physics that

VARIATIONS

FADING/DRAWING

the ball follows this kind of path when the clubface is open to the swingpath at impact (see illustration on p. 20).

You might use a fade to counter the effects of wind, send the ball around an obstacle, stop the ball more quickly, or you might counter the effect of a fairway that slopes from left to right.

To create a fade, open your stance slightly so that your footline is no longer parallel to the target line, but instead points left of the target. Your hips and shoulders should both remain more open to the target than for hitting the ball straight. Aim the clubhead left of the target and make a backswing slightly outside the

target line, and on the downswing keep your hips and clubface opening towards the target as you swing the club across this line. Hold the face open a little longer through impact. Your swingplane will be slightly steeper than usual, and the divot you make will point to the left of the target line.

Drawing the ball

This means hitting the ball in such a way that it moves from right to left as it flies towards the target. This effect is produced when the clubface is closed to the swingpath at impact (see illustration on p. 59).

You would use a draw to counter the effects of wind or a sloping fairway and avoid obstacles. In addition you use draw to make the ball run further. It is more difficult to draw a ball with a short iron because the loft of the club produces a lot of backspin, countering the effect of the sidespin that produces the draw.

To hit a draw, close your stance so that your footline now points slightly right of the target. Your hips and shoulders also remain closed to the target until just before impact and the

Right: The stance is slightly open for the fade, as are the hips and shoulders. The swingpath is slightly out to in. *Far right:* The stance is closed for the draw so that the foot line points slightly right of the target. The hips and shoulders are closed until just before impact.

clubhead path moves from in to out, aiming right of the target. Your swingplane will be slightly flatter than usual and your divot mark will point right of the target.

The effect of a draw is similar to that of topspin in tennis. Some people like to picture the shot as having the same kind of movement as a topspin forehand, so if you have played tennis you might find it helpful in producing a draw.

Punched shots

These are described this way because the swing is not so smooth as usual – hence the 'punch'. Punch shots tend to make the ball fly lower through the air and are therefore particularly useful when playing in windy conditions as the wind has less chance to affect the flight of the ball. You also use a similar technique to hit the ball out of a divot mark or when your ball lies in heavy rough. In these circumstances the way you swing (or punch) the club allows you to get the ball even though you have a bad lie (see pp. 52-3 for text and illustrations).

To produce a punched shot, position the ball back in an open stance. This will cause the club to descend at a steeper angle than usual, allowing the clubface to 'get at' more of the ball despite the difficult lie. Keep your hips opening as you strike the ball to avoid the clubhead turning over too quickly. You will take a much larger divot than on a normal shot because of the steep angle of attack. Beware of trying too hard to keep the ball low; the mechanics of the action will take care of the flight of the ball.

Getting extra height on the ball

Occasionally you will want to get extra height on a shot to clear some trees, or to stop the ball quickly. To do this, move the ball forward in your stance and swing as normal (see illustration). The effect of moving the ball forward in your stance is that when the club meets the ball it is moving parallel to the ground, rather than slightly downwards. The ball is now not only lifted by the loft of the club but also by the shallower movement of the clubhead, so giving it extra height.

Once again, the mechanics of the action will create the extra height. You do not have to 'lift' the ball up.

Adapting the basics to suit the prevailing conditions is one of the hallmarks of a consistent golfer. Bernhard Langer once adapted his swing to enable him to play a shot standing 6ft off the ground – his ball had landed in a tree!

Far left: For a punched shot the ball is positioned back in the stance and the clubhead descends at a steeper angle than usual.
Above: For extra height the ball is moved further forwards in the stance and the shoulders are tilted slightly.

CONSTANT CONFUSION

"My problem with caddies is I have too many shots. When I pull a club out I can make a ball go almost any distance I want. If it's 150 yards I can pull out a 5 iron but the caddie doesn't know if I'm going to punch it, hit a slow fade or what. If it's 180 yards and I pull out a 6 iron, the caddie has no idea if I'm going to bump and run it hard or hook it." – *Lee Trevino*

Royal St. George's posing a problem for Bernhard Langer as he chips to the 9th green in the 1985 British Open.

COMMON ERRORS

THE SLICE

There are seven errors that you are likely to encounter when playing golf - slicing, hooking, topping, duffing, shanking, pushing or pulling and yipping. If you are unlucky enough to be hitting one of these shots, *don't panic*. Even the pros have suffered most of these errors at some time in their careers. When you find yourself making errors, it is vital to respond to them properly and panicking only makes things worse.

Mechanically, there are many things you may be doing that are causing you to produce one of these shots - too many to encompass them all in this book. However, underlying almost all errors there are usually two primary factors:

1. Not understanding clearly the 'physics' of how the club acts on the ball.

2. Failing to 'feel' accurately differences in body and club position.

Both of these can suck you into trying too hard, with all the associated problems. Imagine you are trying to service the engine of your car. If you do not understand how the engine works, it will be pure luck if you do something that actually makes the car run better. It's the same when you try to correct a fault in your shot-making without understanding how the shot is produced. If, when you were servicing your car, you were unable to see the engine parts clearly, again you would be in trouble. This is the same thing as being unable to 'feel' what you are doing accurately when you play golf.

This chapter contains some suggestions as to what might be happening mechanically if you are making one of these errors, but in order to make effective changes you have to increase 'feel'.

Making corrections

The most effective way of making self corrections is to reduce everything to a pace and distance that does not push you into trying too hard. Practise by hitting the ball about 50yd at a very easy pace. Use a half or even quarter swing and make what you do very simple. Hit 50 balls this way, all the time noticing how the shot feels. Use your knowledge of 'the physics' to guide you to the area in your

swing that you have lost touch with and just 'feel' how the club moves without trying to correct anything. Get to know it and trust that your body will adapt. As long as you don't overtighten, and above all, you keep your patience, it will.

There will be some days when you cannot seem to do anything other than make errors, no matter what you do. When this happens all you can do is accept that you are not going to play well, and do the best you can.

The slice

As you can see from the illustration, the slice is an exaggerated form of the fade. The ball moves from left to right so much that it ends up travelling more sideways rather than forwards, so you lose length and end up in trouble on the right. It is caused by your clubhead being too open to the swingpath at impact and your swingpath being too much out to in (see illustration opposite).

The most common reasons for the above happening lie with your fundamental techniques. Your grip may be too weak (see p. 24), making it difficult for you to return the club to the ball with a square clubface. Strengthening the grip should enable you to let the clubface 'release' properly through impact.

By far the most common cause of slicing is the out to in downswing. At the top of your backswing, your right shoulder moves quickly outwards, throwing the clubhead across the target line in a chopping action. This is quite often accompanied by your weight staying on the right side, which will serve to compound the problem.

To cure this, keep your right side (particularly the right shoulder) 'quiet' throughout the

Depending on the alignment of the clubface at impact the two swingpaths shown can produce any of the following results. The in to out swing (blue) is usually associated with the push (A) when the clubface is square to the clubhead path at impact, and the hook (B) when the clubface is closed at impact. The push-fade is produced by an open face at impact combined with the in to out swing. It causes the ball to start right of the target and to spin even further right. The out to in swing (red) is associated with the pull (C) when the clubface is square to the clubhead path at impact, and with the slice (D) when the clubface is open at impact.

When the clubface is closed at impact a pull-hook is produced, which starts the ball left of the target and spins it even further left during flight.

swing. In fact, your shoulders should pause momentarily at the top of the backswing, and your hands and arms should start the downswing while your back is still facing the target. This will ensure that you start your downswing on the inside of the target line and, if combined with a good weight-shift, should alleviate the problem of a slice.

The hook

Just as slicing is an exaggerated form of fading, hooking is an exaggerated form of drawing. Hooking is caused by your clubhead being very closed in relation to the clubhead path and, generally speaking, your swingpath following a line from in to out (see illustration on p. 59).

The causes of these effects are more or less the opposite of the slice. Your grip might be too strong, causing the clubface to be closed at impact, but the chances are your weight is still not moving fast enough to the left side which, combined with an accentuated in to out swingpath, will make the clubhead turn over too quickly. Check first if your grip is too strong and, if it is, make the necessary adjustments (see p. 24). Then make a wider, steeper backswing, and clear your hips towards the hole earlier, pulling your weight over on to the left side and making room for the clubhead to follow through inside the target line.

In correcting the hook or the slice, you will probably need to exaggerate whatever changes you make. This is because you will probably want the 'feel' of your shot to be close to what you are used to, yet this will not often produce the results you want. The new grip or swing may feel strange, but where the ball goes will tell you whether it is effective or not. Remember, unfamiliar is not always uncomfortable.

The top

If you top the ball, the bottom edge of your club has met the ball part of the way up its back, giving it a downward blow (see illustration) which causes it to scuttle along the ground, losing distance. At its worst, the ball only travels a few yards.

Topping often accompanies slicing in that

its common causes are an out to in swingpath and your weight staying on your back foot. These factors cause the club to travel upwards too much as it strikes the ball, forcing the leading edge of the club to make contact. Moving your head up can also have the same effect.

Swinging your club a little more from in to out and moving your weight over to your left side through impact will help to prevent you from topping the ball. Rather than rushing the club in early, let it lag behind and catch up by itself. Topping is what causes the infuriatingly named 'smile' or cut in the cover of the ball – hence the economic advantage of cut-resistant balls for beginners.

The duff

Duffing or hitting 'fat' means that the clubhead has met the ground before reaching the ball (see illustration). The clubhead loses speed and the ball, as a result, does not travel very far. Duffing, at its worst, can be very funny for spectators as the golfer sometimes takes an enormous divot and the ball only moves a few feet – very frustrating for the golfer.

The duff often accompanies the hook as it is caused by an in to out swingpath and, once again, not enough weight-shift from your right side to your left. The ball nearly always finishes to the right of the target.

If you swing with a slightly steeper swingpath and a complete weight shift, holding your head at a constant height, you will contact the ball before the ground.

The shank

The shank is the most dreaded of all shots, where the ball flies almost directly sideways right of the target line. What happens is that the hosel of your club (the part where the shaft meets the blade) makes contact with the ball (see illustration).

The most common causes of shanking are swinging your clubhead in a plane that is too flat, letting your hands move too far away from your body, and adopting too close an address position. Some ways that you might prevent yourself from shanking are by keeping your weight on your heels; by standing further away from the ball at your address position; and by keeping your left arm close to your chest through the downswing.

The push and pull

The push is a shot that flies straight but to the right of the target. The pull is a shot that flies straight but left of the target. Both of these errors are caused by your clubface being square to the path of the clubhead but not square to the target, so a push means you are swinging in to out and a pull means you are swinging out to in.

Alternatively, you may be swinging the club well, but your alignment may be faulty (see text on p. 24).

The yips

Yipping is fortunately not as common as the other errors, but can be an absolute nightmare to anyone experiencing it. Yipping refers to what happens to some people when they are over-anxious when they putt. We have already described putting as a smooth, effortless stroke. A yip occurs when the putter suddenly jerks through the ball, sending it way off-line and much too fast, leaving the ball a long way from the hole.

Yipping is usually caused by over-anxiety. The more worried you are about your putting, the tighter your muscles and the shallower your breathing become. The tighter your muscles are the more difficult it is to control them and your movements become increasingly jerky. When you finally attempt to stroke the ball, you are left with so little control it is as if your arms just 'spasm', and of course the more you jerk at the ball the more anxious you become.

To eliminate the yips you need to do two things. First of all, realize that missing one putt

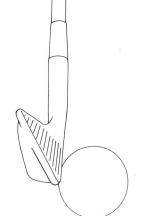

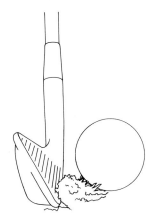

Left: The top. The leading edge of the club meets the ball.
Middle: The shank. The hosel of your club meets the back of the ball, causing it to spin viciously to the right.
Bottom: The duff. The leading edge makes contact with the ground and takes a divot before making contact with the ball.

COMMON ERRORS

is not the end of your score. Second, put all of your attention on breathing out as you stroke the ball, as this diverts your attention from your fear of missing and helps your muscles to relax.

We have separated these errors into different categories, but of course life is not always that convenient. Sometimes you will find yourself combining several of these errors – for exam-

ple, when your ball starts to the right of the target and curves even further to the right of the target, you have a combination of a push and a slice.

The trajectory of the ball can tell you a lot about what happened at impact. It can also tell you where you need to increase your 'feel' and therefore control. But be careful! Knowing what happened at impact is no substitute

Jack Nicklaus wishing he
were 6 inches taller!

for 'feeling' what is actually happening – to suppose otherwise is a very common mistake in learning.

You may have noticed that a common denominator between a lot of these errors is poor weight-shift. This is often caused by a lack of commitment or an unwillingness to trust what you are trying to do, resulting in a half-hearted half attempt! Once you have made up your mind what you want to do, go ahead and swing the club to a full finish, with your weight on the outside of your left foot. The worst that can happen is you will hit a bad shot, which you have done before and will almost certainly do again if you hang back – but less often now! Load, aim, fire! If you're not afraid of the bad shots, the good ones will show up more often.

COURSE MANAGEMENT
MAKING LIFE EASY

The game of golf does not involve a standard playing arena in the way most other sports do. Although tennis is played on four or five different surfaces and the pace of the snooker table may vary slightly from venue to venue, both are games played within set boundaries. In golf, every course is different, and sometimes spectacularly so.

From the desert courses of Central Africa with their sand and oil greens, to the lush, well manicured fairways of America and the wickedly difficult challenge of the windswept British links, each has its own individual attraction. But to play any of them as well as you can, one rule must be obeyed – you must learn to accept your own limitations and quite simply, make the best of what you have got! If you can be aware of, and therefore step over, the early pitfall of trying to hit the perfect shot too often, you can develop your scoring technique well beyond other golfers who see the pros hitting straight at the flag and try to emulate them.

Course management is a skill which you can only develop by getting on the golf course and gaining experience. Inevitably, in the course of gaining experience you will make mistakes, but by learning from these and trying to avoid them in the future you will maximize your chances of scoring well.

The easiest shot

In order to leave yourself the easiest shot possible, always look at a hole from green to tee, noting the position of the flag, and work out the easiest route to it.

If the flag is on the right edge of the green the left half of the fairway will usually leave the easiest shot, and vice versa. Sometimes, on wide open courses, even an adjoining fairway will offer you a more inviting route to the hole.

If the hole is cut near a bunker or water hazard a shot to the middle of the green is very often called for, even for very good players. This is where you must take into consideration your own limitations – that is, how often you hit the ball straight where you want to! Everyone knows that the perfect shot will leave you a simple chance for a birdie, but only *you* know how likely you are to be able to

Laura Baugh making a sand shot look easy at the 1986 Dinah Shore tournament.

COURSE MANAGEMENT

HAZARDS/DOG LEGS/CLUBBING

hit that shot. For every birdie you make you will probably make half a dozen bogies or worse by being aggressive at the wrong time.

Now that you have decided to go for the 'fat' part of the green you should leave yourself the easiest putt possible. This usually means an uphill putt. Obviously if the green slopes towards whatever trouble is beside the flag this will not be possible, but in this case you can use the natural contours to get the ball closer.

In the case of a par 5 hole where it will most likely take you three shots to reach the green, the last of these shots will be the most important. So, as the first two shots are positional, it is important to keep them on the fairway as this determines the difficulty of the third shot. A sensible choice of club off the tee should make your second shot easier, whereas if you try to get as close as possible to the green in two shots with a driver and a 3 wood (as so many players do) you may end up hacking your way through the rough or chipping out of the trees. By playing the hole sensibly, with perhaps a 3 wood off the tee, and a 3 or 4 iron, the green should be easily accessible with your third shot, from the middle of the fairway! Remember, it is going to take you three shots anyway, no matter how hard you hit the first two, so do not be afraid to leave yourself a slightly longer third shot. That way you have given yourself every chance.

Hazards

On some holes you may encounter hazards which are difficult for you to hit over or get past, such as a stream or fairway bunker. Unless you are feeling very confident, you are better off laying up short. A common mistake with laying up is to take too much club. The worry of leaving yourself a very long second shot tends to make you choose a club which, if you hit well, will cause the ball to go just far enough to land you in precisely the hazard you were trying to avoid. (Of course in this instance Murphy's Law is automatically enforced, and you hit the ball very well!)

When you have decided to lay up, choose a club which, even if you hit the ball very solidly, will leave you short of the hazard. There are

few moments more infuriating than when you realize that you would have carried the hazard comfortably had you made a similar contact with the driver!

Dog legs

You will no doubt have encountered many dog leg holes on different courses that you have played. With the dog leg, there is always the temptation to cut off as much of the corner as possible. However, unless there is very little trouble on the corner, such as very short rough, it is nearly always better to be too wide off the tee, rather than too narrow. From too wide you still get a look at the green, albeit if it is a little further away, but from too narrow you can often be blocked out by tall trees or a bad lie. In this case it will usually be all you can do to chop out and land short of the green, while the player who has gone wide still has a chance of reaching it in two. The guideline is if there is room to play with, use it.

Clubbing

Choosing the correct club for the job is an art which can take many obstacles out of the game. For example, if you have a shot of about 150yd to a flag on the front of a green with bunkers on the front right and left, a well-struck 5 iron might carry the correct distance. Alternatively, a slightly mishit 5 iron, a little to the left or right of the hole, may well finish up in one of the bunkers. A nicely struck 4 iron, however, may finish 20-30ft behind the hole, or if it is mishit slightly to the left or right it will finish about level with the flag on the front of the green. By choosing the 4 iron, although it does not seem the 'perfect' club, you give yourself that vital margin for error that can cut shots from your handicap. This is where knowing approximately how far you can hit each club is of great importance. You can learn how far you hit the clubs on the driving range, where there are yardage markers for this purpose, or on the golf course by memorizing landmarks and pacing off how far they are from the middle of the greens.

The modern touring pro not only knows exactly how far he has got between his ball and the hole but how far various hazards are from the tees, enabling him to make decisions on whether or not to lay up or go for the 'carry'. There is no reason why you should not get to know your own course by keeping a notebook of a few simple yardages in your golf bag.

Trouble shots

No matter how wisely or carefully you play, you will often find yourself in positions requiring a recovery shot of some kind. You will

doubtless have seen players such as Ballesteros and Langer performing 'impossible' recoveries from the trees, water and long grass. But they too have had their moments when they have bitten off more than they could chew and ended up making bogies. The main problem of being in trouble is that when faced with two choices you can nearly always convince yourself that the toughest choice is best. When faced with either chipping out sideways on to the fairway or punching a 5 iron through a 6in hole in a rotten tree 20yd away and on to the green (only a slight exaggeration) the choice, the spectator would think, is obvious. Meanwhile, in the back of your mind, a little voice is suggesting otherwise. 'Just think how good it would feel to get it on the green from here,' it whispers. Our advice is: ignore that voice and chip it out sideways! Again, what you are doing here is learning how to score, and for every miracle

An average player would have conceded defeat on a shot like this and picked up the ball. But Sam Torrance was confident that he could get out without penalty and executes this most difficult shot perfectly. Ryder Cup, Belfry, 1986.

COURSE MANAGEMENT

Ballesteros drawing his tee shot around the dog leg of the 12th hole at Wentworth during the World Match Play tournament, 1985.

shot you pull off there are twenty more that land you in worse trouble. That is not to say that there won't be times when you will have to 'have a go' and attempt the usually unthinkable, but limit these to occasions when you feel very confident indeed.

You encounter a similar situation when in a fairway trap. Choosing a club here is very important, as being over-ambitious can mean leaving the ball in the bunker. Make sure that you have chosen a club with enough loft to clear the lip of the bunker. Quite often this will mean that you will not be able to reach the green, but again, better safe than sorry. Maintain your height throughout the swing by holding your chin a little higher so that your head does not dip on the downswing. If you use this technique it will help you to strike the ball before the sand.

Water

At the sight of water, handicap players (and pros!) often tighten up and become neurotic. There is obviously something about the thought of landing in there with a splash that causes more worry than the prospect of ending up in dense trees or bunkers. The problem is that the penalty for ending up in a water hazard can often be more severe than other hazards as the ball is usually completely unplayable (and irretrievable!).

To learn to cope with the extra pressure that a water hazard presents you must try to break down your round into individual shots. In fact, this theory can be applied to any particularly difficult shot. For example, how much importance do you place on each individual shot? If you hit the ball into the water, will it alter the course of world politics? Or will your

wife or husband leave you (if they have not already, because you play too much golf)? Of course not. In reality there are only two possibilities here; you will either hit it in the water, or you will not. If you can make *both* of these two acceptable to you, then you will worry less. When you are not worried about it you are giving yourself the best chance of making a good swing, thus reducing the chances of hitting a bad shot. What more could you ask for? How many times have you heard someone say after a bad shot, 'I *knew* I was going to do that'? This is a remark typical of someone who actually had *no* idea what he or she was going to do, but was not prepared to accept the bad result! If you are going to plan a reaction to a shot, why not make it a positive one irrespective of where the ball goes. You cannot rewind it, so get on with it!

Horses for courses

Although there are many different types of golf course they can generally be split up into two different groups: those where the ball runs a lot, and those where it does not. The former are usually links or heathland courses, although some parkland courses can become just as fast in dry weather. These present a different challenge to the golfer as the ball becomes more difficult to stop, both on the fairways and on the greens. So often you will find yourself having hit a tee shot into the edge of the rough, faced with a shot to a hard, fast green. You will have to work out how far and in which direction the ball will run when it hits the ground. Using the natural contours of the course is another of the seemingly endless challenges that the game presents, particularly when played on the links of the British Isles. No doubt it is a source of endless comfort to the armchair viewer at home that the game can force even the best players in the world to struggle for over-par scores, making them feel exactly the same emotions as any club golfer having a bad day!

Course management, in a nutshell, is accurately assessing what your current ability is, and then making the most of it! It sounds easier than it is, and of course, if it were that easy, the game would not be so much fun.

PLAYING WITH YOUR HEAD

"I partnered Jack Nicklaus in a tournament in Hawaii in 1974. He had a lousy round but he was one under par for the day and he won because he managed his game and the course so well. He was conservative because he knew he had to be." – *Hale Irwin, twice US Open Champion.*

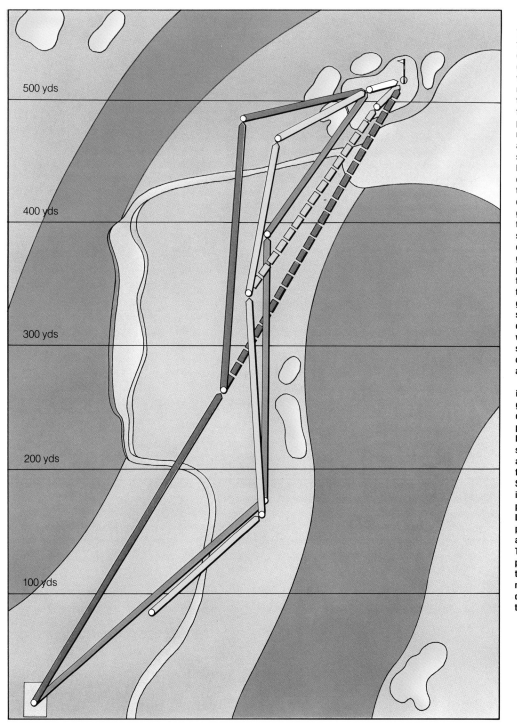

500 yds

400 yds

300 yds

200 yds

100 yds

The illustration shows how three players of different capabilities might play a difficult par 5 hole safely and well. The red line denotes the route the pro might take, and the yellow and blue lines are female and male handicap players respectively. Both the man and woman have chosen a club for the tee shot that is sufficient to carry the stream but will not take them far enough to reach the bunker, thus taking one of the hazards out of play completely. As the green is out of reach for all but the longest of hitters a safety shot is now the obvious choice, setting up a chance to go for the flag. This shot is played to the right half of the fairway, taking no risks with the water short or right of the green. Most of the hazards are short of the flag, so a good decision for the third shot would be to take a club that, if slightly mishit, would still carry at least to the front edge, as both our players have done.

The pro, on the other hand, is long enough to reach the green in two shots. However, depending on how well he is playing and on the lie of his ball, he may choose to lay up safely (solid line) or have a go at the green (broken line). The female has a similar option. She can either go for the green in three shots (broken line) or play it safe and take four. Laying up leaves a very simple pitch shot, which should leave a realistic chance of a birdie. The club required will also play a big part in the choice of the second shot. Most pros are not fond of attacking a dangerously guarded green if they have to hit a wooden club.

COMPETITION AND COMPETING

MIND GAME

One point of view says that competition is good for you because it builds character. Another says that competition is bad for you as it fosters aggression and conflict. Both of these can be true. You have probably seen competition bring out the worst in people in both the amateur and professional game. Gone is the pleasant, good-humoured individual you were with in the clubhouse. Present instead is a cursing, club throwing, bad-tempered complainer, walking around the course with his or her head engulfed in their own personal black cloud. But you will also have seen people who, when competing, seem to find greater abilities. They concentrate harder, raise their game and thrive under circumstances that seem nightmarish to others.

So, what is it about competition that inhibits some golfers and inspires others? Well, the subject would provide enough material for a book on its own, but let's look at several aspects of competition that occur repeatedly at all levels in the game.

Pressure, nerves and the fear of failure

You experience pressure and become nervous when your mind is full of doubt and concern about whether or not you will, or can, achieve the result you want. You will notice that you are able to watch other golfers compete without feeling nervous or pressured, and they can watch you competing likewise (of course, if you care a lot about whether a particular player wins you may experience pressure as a spectator). So, pressure is engendered by you and not by the circumstances. You create it by allowing your attention to wander off what you are doing. What it wanders on to are things such as how well or badly you are doing, trying to impress others, and the difficulty of the shot. But most of all, what can claim your attention is the fear of failure – of failing to achieve what you want. It is this fear that will actually cause you to fail, and failing is the very thing you are afraid of. Failure is a problem when you see it as being bad. If you can see something beneficial come out of it, you will not be afraid – but more of that later.

The important thing to understand about pressure is that you and only you create it, and thus you and only you can reduce it. One way to do this is to discipline your attention and put as much of it as you can on the here and now, on what you *are* actually doing. Find something easy to pay attention to and concentrate on that. Every time your mind wanders away, gently bring it back.

It bears restating that concentrating on breathing can be very helpful, as your breathing will become shallower as you experience pressure.

The golden rule is to get your attention away from your fears of the future and on to the present, *any* part of the present, even if it's the trees and sky!

Why compete?

Sometimes an understanding of why you are competing will help to make it an enjoyable experience. First of all, understand that competition means you are out to beat someone. This factor is sometimes disguised in golf because you don't often directly oppose someone, except in match play (of course it's possible to merely play the course and ignore your fellow competitors). Other sports highlight the adversarial nature of competing much more graphically. In tennis you are deliberately trying to make life difficult for your opponent, and in boxing you are out to injure him. Even in golf, you are aiming to do better than everyone else. So, why do it? What do you gain?

Some people hold the view that competition builds character. When you compete you can gain the reward of winning or having your best score in an event and so on. These factors occur after the competition. What is often missed is that as you compete you improve, provided you keep a positive and long-term

Greg Norman smiling his way to victory during the 1986 British Open at Turnberry.

PERSPECTIVES

'Please, please go in' – Tom Kite at the 6th hole during the final round of the US Masters at Augusta, 1986.

approach to what you are doing. It is the ultimate test of your ability. The more often you take the test, the better you get at it.

Let's make an analogy. If you wish to strengthen your arm muscles, you lift weights. You start with a 10lb weight and lift that for a few weeks, then move on to a 15lb weight, and so on. The more repetitions you do, the stronger you get. Competing is the extra weight – the more repetition you do, the stronger you become mentally *provided* that your repetitions are of high quality – that is, you stay relaxed and positive.

In the end you might ask yourself what you gain personally from competing. If you cannot enjoy it the majority of the time, then why do it? You can still play the game without going through the agonies that people sometimes suffer.

Many people confuse the importance of competition with the importance of real life. Temporarily the game has become 'real' and they behave as if the situation had huge amounts of money resting on it, or even life or death. They have forgotten that golf is a game. It is much more fun if it is played *as if* it is real, but at the same time remembering that it *is* only a game and that the sun does not fall out of the sky when you lose.

Errors and excuses

When you make an error, it is yours and no-one else's. Blaming somebody moving, or a noise, or your putter, is avoiding the issue. Some people also blame their grip or their backswing and sometimes this is also an excuse (obviously it can also be an accurate diagnosis of what went wrong). In the end you and no-one else are responsible for what you do. If you want things to change, you must change. If you want to swing differently, you have to try out a different feel and cope with all the errors and anxiety in doing something new and strange. If you want to keep calm and not lose your temper when you hit a bad shot, *you* have to stop doing whatever it is that causes you to lose your temper.

If someone coughs as you are about to hit the ball and you mishit, it is your responsibility. Of course, you are not responsible for them

PERSEVERING TO PERFECTION

coughing, but you are for the way you react to their cough. It is your responsibility to train your concentration to the point where someone coughing will not disturb you.

Perfection

One of the greatest obstacles to a good score is trying to hit every shot perfectly. Perfection, of course, is a wonderful goal to strive for, but it is rarely attained, and you do not have to hit the ball perfectly to make a good score. So many golfers go around shaking their heads and muttering about how they should have done this or that. They fail to understand that the professionals only hit the ball perfectly five or six times a round. If you can attain that level of perfection you will be doing well. The unrealistic pursuit of perfection can create much unnecessary pressure. You do not have to have a perfect strike to have a perfect score. At its extreme, you could zig zag your way down the fairway and get the ball in the hole in par. When you compete you are judged by how many shots you took, not by how perfect your strike was and how well you executed your swing.

So give yourself a break. You might never be perfect, but you can keep progressing, and make good scores as you do.

Giving up

Golf's scoring system, in stroke play, usually means that every single shot counts. If you drop a shot at a hole it counts against you, whereas most other sports give you room to recover. Some people are prone to give up once they have dropped one or two shots. If you think that as soon as you have dropped a shot you have no chance of winning, you are forgetting two important things:

1. Other competitors are probably dropping shots as well, which means that you might still be in with a very good chance.

2. You *can* recover shots in golf. Watch professionals play. It is not that they never make errors that makes them so good. They hit the ball into trouble and 3-putt sometimes. It is the way they recover that makes them good. Even in their best rounds they have bogies; they just have many more birdies.

When you drop a shot on a given hole, you can actually get it back on a later hole, provided you don't give up.

Remember the game is not over until the last shot is played. Many players with seemingly impenetrable leads have squandered them on the last few holes. Equally, other players have come from nowhere on the back 9 to snatch victory. So hang in there no matter what the score.

Playing to win – the killer instinct

You have got to have the 'killer instinct' to succeed in sport. Whether this is true or not, we can say that you do have to be very single-minded and you have to play to win as opposed to playing not to lose.

When you play not to lose, you become defensive, negative and too careful. It makes you much more prone to over-tightening your muscles and making more errors. Of course, so does the other extreme – playing recklessly and over aggressively.

For most golfers, playing positively (not recklessly) to win gives them their best chance of producing a good shot, and it is a much more satisfying way to play.

To compete in any sport, you have to be mentally tough. You must be able to control your physical, mental and emotional reactions. It is a skill that can be practised, most of the time in the heat of competition, but the benefits can reach out beyond your sport. If you learn to toughen up mentally in your golf, you can use that toughness in any activity outside the game.

Golf is a game of precision. It does not tolerate extremes. You cannot easily take your frustration out on the ball because of the dangers of over-tightening. Even your manners and behaviour in golf have to be kept

Sally Little daring the ball not to go close to the flag stick!

within well defined limits, hence there is very little bad sportsmanship or unruly crowd behaviour. It demands high levels of self control, particularly during the stress of competition.

In summary, competition can be fun and very beneficial, reaching out beyond your golf. But even if competing is not for you, there is still plenty in the sport for you to enjoy.

AFTERTHOUGHTS

The week before I was introduced to Alan, I was seriously considering giving up golf. I had missed 9 of the last 11 cuts by a single shot, and was down to my father's last fifty quid. The week after I was introduced to Alan I shot 64 in the first round of the Irish P.G.A. Championship and led the tournament to the 72nd hole. On the tee I was struck by the difficulty of the shot awaiting me. A little voice inside my head was saying, 'Where's the fairway?'. Out of bounds left on the practice ground, and out of bounds right on the railway line. Needless to say, the panic button was found and pushed. I wanted to avoid the 5.45 from Dublin, so I snap hooked the ball on to the practice ground. I took 7 and lost the tournament by a shot. Strangely, though, I was quite relieved in a way, as I felt that I had discovered something. I had been so worried about the possibility of hooking it on to the practice ground or slicing it on to the railway line that I'd tensed up and hit it on to the practice ground to justify having worried about it in the first place! The answer was simple. Don't worry about it.

I'm still trying not to worry about it. Sometimes I can do it, and win tournaments and a lot of money. I'm hoping to get better at it, with more practice. Give it a go.

David Feherty

Once you are armed with more information about the game, or perhaps a different point of view, then comes the task of putting it into practice.

Timothy Gallwey, who wrote the *Inner Game* books, once said to me 'Alan, in a way it's about trusting yourself'. He encouraged me to play games as if I had lots of ability instead of very little. I found that when I trusted myself in this way I worried less, learned faster, and played better. Of course, I have not yet won the Open, but I do play better than I thought I could and enjoy both playing and competing immensely.

As you put the lessons in this book to work, take a tip from Gallwey. Trust yourself. You almost certainly underestimate what you are capable of.

In America they have an expression: 'Let the good times roll'. My wish for you and I is that they roll into the hole – in one!

Alan Fine

78